Coping with Behavior Change in Dementia:

A Family Caregiver's Guide

Beth Spencer and Laurie White

This handbook is written in honor of the many hundreds of family members we have had the privilege of working with over the past three decades. Your courage, steadfastness and problem-solving abilities continue to inspire us. Most of what is included in this book, we have learned from you.

Special thanks to Tom White who put in many hours editing, raising questions, keeping us in line and becoming an expert in behaviors and dementia.

©Whisppub LLC

March 2015

Visit Whisppub.com for book ordering information.

TABLE OF CONTENTS

TABLE OF CONTENTS

TABLE OF CONTENTS

TABLE OF CONTENTS

ABOUT THE AUTHORS

Beth Spencer

Laurie White

Beth Spencer and Laurie White

We have been working in the field of dementia care since the early 1980s. We have worked in private practice, in adult day programs, assisted living communities, and in medical clinics. During these 30 years or so, we have had the privilege of speaking to and working with thousands of family members who are caring for someone with memory loss. Most of the ideas in this book have come from families. We stand in awe of the energy, the courage, and the wisdom that families have shown us.

We are the authors of **Moving a Relative with Memory Loss: A Family Caregivers Guide** (available on Amazon.com. For bulk orders, contact us at whisppub.com). We are also two of the three authors of **Understanding Difficult Behaviors**, which was originally published by Eastern Michigan University in 1989 (now out of print). Our colleague and co-author, Anne Robinson, contributed a great deal over the years to our thinking about behavioral issues and dementia care. This book grows out of our long collaboration with her and with other colleagues to whom we give our thanks for their tireless efforts to make the world a better, easier place for people who have cognitive losses, and for their families.

INTRODUCTION

Gerald Pitts was 83 years old when he began to have some difficulty with his memory. At first, it did not impact his life too much, but as his disease progressed, he needed increasing amounts of supervision and help with daily life. As he needed more help, his wife Josephine also felt like she needed more help understanding his behavior and how to respond to it in the most caring and appropriate ways.

Understanding dementia behaviors that challenge family and professional caregivers is never easy. This handbook is intended to help families understand possible causes of common behavior changes and learn to respond more effectively to behaviors such as repetitive actions, agitation, incontinence and sleep problems. It is our firm belief that many of the most challenging behaviors may be minimized when caregivers learn how to identify root causes and try strategies that are known to help some people with dementia much of the time. We, like most professionals in the dementia field, consider medication intervention for behavior change to be a last resort. There are usually unwanted side effects of medications. By using many of the strategies outlined in this handbook, many families have been able to avoid using medications to treat behaviors. However, we recognize that at times medications are necessary.

This book is based on the premise that we all have basic human needs, including to be loved, comforted, to be productive members of our community and to feel as though we belong. We all need emotional warmth and a sense of identity. These needs are no different for someone living with cognitive loss. Individuals with dementia may feel like they don't belong or may have a need for social and physical contact and sensory stimulation. The brain changes that cause dementia can affect a person's ability to recognize, express and resolve these needs independently and often times the environment is inadequate to address these needs.

Another basic right of all people is to be described as who we are and not by the symptoms of a disease, in this case some form of dementia. In this book you will read about "a person who walks away," not a "wanderer." We believe that changing the words we use can influence our attitudes and expectations in a positive way that benefits both caregivers and the person with dementia.

About This Handbook

Gender references: Throughout the handbook we have used female pronouns for ease of reference. There are more women with dementia in the older population, because women live longer and age is a risk factor for many forms of dementia. We recognize that there are, of course, many men with dementia as well.

Caregiver vs. care partner: We have used both terms in this handbook as different people identify with different terms. This book is written for any person who is identified as family, whether spouse, child, partner, dear friend or other.

Case vignettes: We have included short stories throughout the book to illustrate how families have handled certain situations. Although these stories are based on real situations, the names have been changed. We hope that these case studies will help you know the range of feelings other care partners have experienced and how they have handled certain behavioral challenges.

Resources: There is an extensive resource section at the end of this handbook with books, websites, and other information, including national organizations for different forms of dementia, where families may be able to get more detailed information.

Glossary: We have added a glossary at the end with definitions of many of the terms found in this handbook.

Alzheimer's Association 24 Hour Helpline: The Alzheimer's Association serves families with all types of dementia, not just Alzheimer's disease. One of their services is a 24/7 Helpline that "provides reliable information and support to all those who need assistance. Call toll-free anytime day or night at 1.800.272.3900." (alz.org). Many caregivers have found this a helpful resource during a particularly difficult moment with a relative.

Terminology and Types of Dementia

There have been many changes in the past 20 years or so in our understanding of the brain and the sophistication of the diagnostic process. New technologies and brain research have resulted in being able to diagnose and differentiate various types of dementia, but it often remains a complex and lengthy process.

There is not space in this handbook to go into detail about diagnostic procedures and the differentiation of the many kinds of dementia. We've included references and a glossary at the end that may be helpful for understanding more about the diagnostic process and specific diseases. In general, the strategies included in this handbook are such that they apply to different types of dementia. Our suggestions have much more to do with understanding the individual and her behaviors and tailoring strategies to address them.

Below is a very cursory description of the most common types of cognitive disorders in older adults which have been identified as of this writing.

Subjective memory complaints is a recently introduced term to describe the condition where individuals experience memory or cognitive changes in themselves that are too subtle to be picked up by diagnostic testing. Current research cannot tell us whether subjective memory complaints are a good predictor of dementia in the future.

Mild cognitive impairment (MCI) or **Mild Neurocognitive Disorder** is relatively recent terminology used to identify people with mild cognitive changes who are not functionally impaired enough to meet the criteria for dementia. "In MCI, cognitive changes are more substantial than those seen in normal aging, but not severe enough to cause major lifestyle changes... It is important to know that, although there can be progression along the continuum from normal aging to MCI to dementia, this does not always occur." (Anderson, Murphy, & Troyer, pp 4-5) MCI is categorized according to whether memory is the main problem (amnestic MCI) or some other cognitive domain, such as language, judgment or decision-making difficulties (non-amnestic MCI).

Dementia is an "umbrella" term used to describe a collection of symptoms rather than the name of a specific disease. Symptoms of dementia can be caused by numerous treatable conditions including urinary tract infection, side effect of medications, vitamin deficiencies, dehydration, etc. Dementia can also be caused by one or more brain disorders that create difficulty in various cognitive areas which may include memory, attention, problem-solving, language, motivation, social behavior and other areas. With a progressive neurological disease such as the ones below, people will eventually have increasing difficulty with daily functioning. The important thing to understand is that there are more than 80 identified diseases that can cause these changes in the brain. Another, recent term for dementia is Major Neurocognitive Disorder.

The various forms of dementia are not considered to be mental illness. The progressive dementias mentioned here are neurological diseases. Some people may have a mental illness, such as major depression or bipolar disease, as well as dementia.

Changes in the brain that are caused by a neurological disease can take many forms. These changes can affect a person's memory (**amnesia**); ability to recognize objects and what to do with them (**agnosia**); difficulty using or comprehending language (**aphasia**); difficulty with motor coordination (**apraxia**). A person with apraxia knows what to do, but the moment she begins to focus consciously on the movement, she experiences difficulties. There can also be changes in executive function, which refers to higher level thinking, such as decision-making, judgment, the ability to initiate activities, or to think abstractly, for example, to understand and tell time.

Mixed dementia is a term sometimes given when a person has more than one type of dementia, for example Alzheimer's disease and vascular dementia. The presence of multiple disease processes can make diagnosis difficult.

Alzheimer's disease is the most common cause of progressive dementia. It is estimated that somewhere between 50-75% of those with dementia have Alzheimer's disease. It becomes more prevalent and the risk increases with each decade of age. Early onset Alzheimer's is a term given to people who are diagnosed under the age of 60; early onset is rare. The hallmark of Alzheimer's disease is memory loss, which is nearly always the first symptom. It begins gradually and subtly and is a progressive neurological disease. The speed of progression varies greatly from individual to individual, though symptoms increase in severity over time. Many other symptoms occur during the progression of Alzheimer's disease, including word-finding, difficulty with judgment and decision-making, problem-solving and reasoning abilities; in later stages people often develop difficulty with mobility, continence and other physical problems.

Parkinson's disease (PD) is a progressive neurological disease, typically characterized by changes in motor functions, such as tremor, mobility problems, slowness and lack of facial expression. Eventually many people who have PD experience cognitive changes and are considered to have Parkinson's with dementia.

Lewy Body disease (LBD) has become a common dementia diagnosis in the past 20 years and is considered by some to be the second most common cause of progressive dementia. Early symptoms often include some Parkinsonian symptoms (such as those listed under PD above), hallucinations, large fluctuations from day to day in alertness and functioning, impairment in visuospatial abilities, and changes in decision-making and judgment. LBD and PD with dementia appear to have some overlapping features. Physicians and researchers sometimes say that if the movement problems occur first, then it is PD; if the cognitive changes occur first, then it is LBD. Individuals with LBD often have increased sensitivity to some medications.

Vascular dementia is cognitive impairment that results from changes in the blood vessels of the brain – cerebrovascular disease. This type of disease results in multiple small strokes in the brain that cause dementia symptoms. Changes in attention, judgment and decision-making, and speed of thinking are often present. Vascular dementia is often present with Alzheimer's disease. The major risk factors for vascular dementia are hypertension, heart disease, smoking and diabetes. Treatment involves controlling risk factors as much as possible.

Frontotemporal dementias (FTD) are progressive neurological disorders that primarily affect the frontal and temporal lobes of the brain (forehead and side of head). They tend to occur in younger people, with the majority of cases showing up in individuals between 45 and 65. There are several forms of FTD, one that is characterized primarily by language problems (aphasia) and another that is characterized by significant changes in behavior and personality.

These brief definitions are presented here to help with terminology. In the reference section of this handbook, we have listed books and websites that can provide more in-depth information. It is important that diagnoses be made by medical personnel with experience in geriatrics, neurology, neuropsychology, and/or psychiatry. Although specialists are now much better able to make accurate diagnoses than they were when we wrote Understanding Difficult Behaviors in 1989, it can still be an extremely complex process – especially when individuals present with mixed or rare forms of dementia.

Beth Spencer & Laurie White

References

Alzheimer's Association, (2014). Alzheimer's Disease Facts and Figures. Alzheimer's & Dementia, Volume 10, Issue 2.

American Psychiatric Association, (2013). Diagnostic and Statistical Manual of Mental Disorders (5th ed.). Arlington, VA: American Psychiatric Publishing

Anderson, ND, Murphy, KJ, & Troyer, AK (2012). Living with Mild Cognitive Impairment. Oxford: Oxford University Press.

Budson, AE & Solomon, PR (2011). Memory Loss: A Practical Guide for Clinicians. Elsevier Saunders.

Whitworth, HB & Whitworth, J (2011). A Caregiver's Guide to Lewy Body Dementia. New York: DemosHealth.

TALKING WITH YOUR RELATIVE

5

TALKING WITH YOUR RELATIVE

Communication is the way we exchange information. It is also how we interact, build a relationship and connect emotionally with another person. To maintain the connection with your relative when her language abilities diminish can be challenging. The changes in communication skills caused by dementia can be frustrating for both the person with memory loss and a care partner.

Care partners react to communication changes in different ways:

"My wife was a librarian and words were her skill. When she began to lose her ability to express herself, we were both heartbroken. I feel like our relationship is much less than it used to be."

"We were not emotionally connecting when my husband began to have problems talking with me. It was hard for me to change the way I had talked to him for nearly 50 years, but I did and I feel much closer to him now."

As Alzheimer's disease and other forms of dementia progress, changes occur in a person's ability to express herself in words. These changes can vary from person to person, depending on how the "language centers" of the brain are affected. Language changes occur differently in different forms of dementia. The examples below are most typical of Alzheimer's disease. For some people, communication changes take place during the earlier stages of dementia and for others in the later stages.

Our belief is that behavior in individuals with dementia is often a form of communication. In other sections of this book, we have offered suggestions on how to respond to specific behaviors, and some communication issues and strategies, including what to say or not say. In this section, we expand our discussion to include some of the communication challenges we hear most often from people with dementia in the earlier stages and from care partners in the later stages. Additional information on communication can be found in many of the books listed in our resource list.

Here are some common changes and suggestions of what to try if you notice these changes in your relative:

Common Communication Changes in the Early Stages

A person's language abilities may not appear to be so different and overall she may be able to communicate quite well early in the disease process. However, there may be some changes that can cause your relative to feel embarrassed and insecure participating in a conversation. Knowing these common experiences can assist you in helping your relative.

Unable to find the right words.

She may substitute a word or several words for the forgotten word. It is common for people to begin to lose the names of things (nouns) in early stages of Alzheimer's disease. For example, when she can't find her checkbook, she might say something like, *"Where's that thing where I write on the piece of paper to pay the bills?"*

- Wait. Give her a chance to come up with the word. It may take longer than you think. Ask your relative, *"Do you want some help with that word?"* Or offer the word that you think your relative may have forgotten. Some people will appreciate this; others may become irritated or frustrated.

> *Ina was talking with her daughter about what she did that day. "After Jeff and I had breakfast, we went to the.... place where you go to get things to help you feel better." Her daughter asked if she went to the pharmacy to get her prescriptions and Ina said, "Yes, that's the place!"*

Loses her train of thought. The ability to pay attention and focus on the conversation diminishes.

- Remind her about what was being discussed, repeating the last words that she used. Some people appreciate having the blank filled in and others may find it irritating.

Thinking and processing language slows down. Some people may withdraw from conversations and social events because they cannot keep up.

- Speak slower, even if you think you are not talking very fast.
- Pause between sentences.
- Try not to speak in long sentences.
- Speak simply but in an adult voice.

Does not comprehend as well as previously. Sometimes the ability to comprehend language is impaired; in other people it may be intact for a long time.

- Use the same strategies: speak slower, etc.
- Repeat the information using the same words if she does not seem to understand.
- Repeat using different words if the above does not work.
- Use visual cues like pointing.

May be easily distracted by multiple conversations, loud noises or activities.
- Try to minimize distractions in the nearby area.

> *Joe had a difficult time talking with Sally, his daughter, when they were sitting on the patio. His daughter suspected that the noise of the nearby traffic was affecting her dad's ability to concentrate on what he wanted to say as well as what she was saying. She suggested to her dad that they go inside to talk. Once inside, Joe was speaking in more fluent sentences and could respond better to what Sally was saying.*

Common Communication Changes as Dementia Progresses

Communication becomes more difficult. The ability to speak and to understand what others are saying usually diminishes.

Fewer words are spoken. As the ability to speak becomes more affected by the changes in the brain, some people have full or partial recognition that their ability to speak is impaired and may withdraw and become silent.

- Watch for signs of depression. Not being able to speak can be terribly frustrating.

- Ask questions that can be answered with "yes" or "no".

- Do not exclude your relative from conversations based on her inability to speak.

A person may make sounds. She may begin humming or whistling.

- Try to understand that this is due to brain damage and the person with dementia may not be able to stop making sounds.

- Determine if the sounds are signs that your relative is distressed, feeling scared or abandoned. If so, try:

  - Playing some favorite, calming music.

  - Giving her something to hold: a doll, quilt, ball, etc.

  - Checking if your relative may be in physical pain. If so, take her to the doctor.

  - Moving to a different environment. Often sounds can be a response to being overwhelmed by too much noise, activity or people.

  - Sitting with her and massage her hands (if you know she is receptive to touch). It can feel comforting to have you nearby.

  - Reassuring her that she is safe.

Confabulation may become more common. Confabulation is making up facts or stories to fill in the gaps in memory. This is not usually a conscious decision, but is something the person's brain does to try to make sense of a world that is not making sense anymore.

> *When the air filter on the furnace made chirping noises, Harry would always say, "There goes that little bird again." No matter how many times his son told him it was the furnace, Harry continued to believe that it was a bird. That was how his brain made sense of a noise that he didn't understand.*

When You Don't Understand What Your Relative is Saying

- Let her know you are listening to her. Often times responding with a simple statement can make someone in the later stages feel acknowledged.

  - *"That's very interesting."*

  - *"Thank you for sharing that with me."*

  - *"I didn't know that."*

- Focus on how your relative may be feeling. Facial expressions and the tone of voice can often convey how she is feeling and be more important than the facts of what she is saying.

  - *"You look sad. Are you feeling sad?"*

  - *"I can see that you are confused by that."*

- If she is talking faster than usual, it may indicate that she is excited or agitated by something. Or her furrowed brow may show you that she is angry.

- *"I can tell by your voice that you are really excited. Am I right?"*
- *"You look angry. I am so sorry. I will help you in any way I can."*

- Focus on one word or phrase. You may be able to decipher what she is trying to say.

- *"Bread. I hear you saying bread, Mary. Are you hungry?"*

- Repeat what you think she is saying.

- Acknowledge how frustrating it is for her and for you when you don't understand what she is trying to say.

- *"I'm sorry I don't understand what you are trying to say. This is hard for me too."*

- Take a break. Involve her in another activity if she continues to be upset. Ask her to go for a walk with you, offer a snack, look at photo albums together, etc.

- Give her a hug, if she likes to be reassured in this way.

When Your Relative Does Not Understand What You Are Saying

- Keep in mind that many people in the later stages of dementia have moments of clarity and can understand and respond to what is being said. For this reason, you should not talk about your relative in front of her or discuss upsetting things in front of her. Never assume that she does not understand.

- Repeat what you said, word for word. Saying it again using the same words, may help. If this doesn't work, try saying it another way.

- Speak slowly and keep it short.

- Show your relative what you are asking her to do. Visual cues sometimes help.

- Change the subject or involve your relative in an activity. Resume the conversation later, if necessary.

- Try silence. It is often what someone needs after putting energy into trying to understand.

Things to Avoid Doing

- Avoid asking questions that rely on memory. Instead of saying, *"Mom who is this in this picture?"* try, *"I know this is you in this photo, but I am not sure who that man is."*

- Don't start a sentence with *"Do you remember?"* Although this is a common question to ask in everyday conversation, it can make a person with dementia feel like a failure when she doesn't remember.

- Don't argue if your relative talks about something that is not true. Many people with dementia have a different reality or orientation to time. Arguing and correcting generally do not work and often result in anger and frustration.

Hector frequently told a story about traveling to Costa Rica with his sister. Many times Anita, his wife, would correct him and remind him that he had gone with her, not his sister. This usually made him angry as his memory was of being there with his sister. Anita learned that she never won the argument, that they both ended up mad and that it was much better just to let Hector tell the story his way.

- Avoid "testing" her. Some families have suggested that it might help their relatives' memories if they test them with memory questions. Also, some families do it to see how well the memory is working. In our experience, this generally makes someone with memory loss feel inadequate and humiliated.

Other Considerations for Talking with Your Relative

- Use your relative's name and identify yourself before you speak if she is not always sure who you are. *"Hi mom, it's me, Victoria."*

- Be sure you are in your relative's field of vision before you start talking. Otherwise you may startle her.

- Ask questions which require a "yes" or "no" answer if decisions have become difficult. Instead of asking, *"What music would you like to listen to now?"* try asking *"Would you like to listen to Bing Crosby now?"* This allows her to make a decision and be involved in the conversation, without putting her on the spot.

- Try to be patient and supportive. People with dementia often put a great deal of energy into trying to speak and understand. Give your relative time to express herself and to process what is being said.

When words fail to be understood, try another form of communication that offers reassurance, love and support: holding her hand, rubbing her arm or back or sitting quietly by her side. Many times our presence is felt more than words.

BECOMING A DETECTIVE: A PROBLEM-SOLVING APPROACH

BECOMING A DETECTIVE:
A PROBLEM-SOLVING APPROACH

One of the challenges of caring for someone with dementia is trying to understand changes in behavior that are causing distress – either to you or to your relative or both. Professionals in dementia care have talked for decades about the need to become a detective in order to understand and respond to the behavior.

This approach is based on the belief that the behavior changes we see in people with dementia are an attempt to communicate something – a need (for example, thirst), discomfort (for example, pain), a feeling (for example, frustration) or something else. Even though the person may be able to still talk, she may have lost the ability to express in words what she needs or is feeling. As a result, her behavior is telling us her need or feeling and it is up to us to understand it. We become behavior detectives.

When an individual is pacing, or wringing her hands or moaning, for example, it is our job to figure out what that behavior is trying to communicate. This handbook was written with that in mind. We have categorized some of the possible causes of a particular behavior and then listed possible strategies for preventing or coping with it. If we don't understand the cause(s) of a behavior, we will have difficulty coming up with appropriate strategies for addressing it.

It can be very helpful to keep a simple record or log of a challenging behavior over several days. By doing this, you may be able to identify a pattern to the behavior that will help you figure out the cause. Below we have given you a case study that includes a behavior log that helped Ann's husband understand what was causing Ann to act and react in certain ways. Throughout this handbook we have suggested that you keep a simple log as one strategy for trying to get to the root cause of behavior.

Ann's Agitation

Ann was diagnosed with Alzheimer's disease 5 years ago. Her husband George has been caring for her alone in their home where they have lived for many years. Ann is self-sufficient in eating and toileting, but needs reminders and assistance to shower. She does not like to change her clothes and has been wearing the same clothes for the past several weeks.

Ann sleeps for approximately 15 hours a day, going to bed around 7:30 PM and getting out of bed between 10 and 10:30 AM the next morning. Mornings are usually the calmest time of the day. Their routine is to go out for breakfast to the nearby bakery where they have a pastry, coffee and juice. They split a sandwich for lunch around 1 PM along with ice tea and a cookie. George says that Ann has developed *"a real sweet tooth"* and won't eat much else besides cookies, candy and ice cream. He controls the sweets by locking them in the pantry.

Lately Ann has become very agitated in the mid-afternoon. She walks around their home, screaming at her husband, pounding on the table and walls and goes in and out of the kitchen slamming cupboard doors. Ann has hit George several times when he approached her to try to calm her.

George says this is the most difficult time of day and he finds it helpful to *"hibernate in my office and read, pay bills or do anything to keep me from yelling at her."* He admits that often Ann's agitation gets to him and he shouts, *"SHUT UP."* He knows this is not right but says he cannot help himself.

With encouragement from a fellow caregiver, George decided to keep a behavior log to see if it would shed any light on Ann's behavior.

WHEN	WHO WAS THERE?	WHERE & WHAT WAS GOING ON?	WHAT WAS THE BEHAVIOR?	WHAT I TRIED & WHAT HAPPENED
Saturday, 3 PM	I was with Ann	Watching TV with me in my office while I read a book.	Anger and agitation	I yelled at her. She yelled back and threatened to hit me.
Sunday, 2 PM	I was with Ann	We were in my office. I left Ann sitting on the sofa and moved to work at my desk.	Ann became upset and started pacing.	I ignored her, but Ann became more agitated and started crying.
Monday, 4 PM	I was with Ann	I was taking a nap in our bedroom.	Ann became upset and yelled at me because I would not get up.	I asked Ann to lie down with me. I stroked her back and she calmed down for a short while.

Things to Consider

As we put on our detective hats, this behavior log gives us some information and some ideas of why Ann might be acting this way. What is Ann's behavior trying to tell us? What might George do to help Ann?

There is a consistent pattern related to time of day. Mid-afternoon is difficult for Ann. We need to think about possible reasons for this.

Ann may be feeling alone and insecure. She wants George's attention. George does not understand that Ann's behavior is a symptom of how she is feeling. He is finding her behavior so stressful that he reacts by yelling at her, which only escalates Ann's anger and agitation.

It may help George to know that agitation and anger are caused by the disease, and the person – in this case Ann – is not able to control her behavior.

Ann may be looking for something to do. While George is occupied with his office work, she may be bored and not know what to do or how to start an activity.

George might try planning an activity that Ann could do and find enjoyable: washing dishes, looking at a photo album of their family vacations, dusting, etc. Going for a drive or taking a walk before mid-afternoon when Ann's agitation usually begins may help. It is often easier to prevent a behavior by changing a routine rather than responding to the behavior once it has begun.

The TV might have upset her. On one occasion the TV was on. What was playing? Was there something on the TV that she might have misunderstood or misinterpreted? Could she be confusing TV with reality?

George could take a closer look at what type of TV Ann is watching. News programs that report violence or disturbing events, action or 'thriller' shows, may be difficult for Ann and cause her distress.

Her sugar craving may be increasing her agitation. An increase in craving sweets is not uncommon for people with dementia. This is largely due to changes in the brain.

Although George is doing what he thinks is best for Ann – locking up sweets – giving Ann an afternoon snack of yogurt, fruit or a cup of cocoa, may help reduce her uncontrollable cravings for sweets and reduce her agitation.

Ann may simply be hungry. She has not eaten much for breakfast or for lunch.

Starting the day with toast, eggs or cereal or something with less sugar may sustain Ann longer. He could try giving Ann a larger lunch: a whole sandwich, for example. George could also document whether eating larger meals affects Ann's level of agitation in the afternoon. Or he could try giving Ann a snack a couple hours after breakfast, rather than waiting 3 or more hours.

What beverages is Ann drinking? We know she has coffee for breakfast and tea for lunch.

If Ann is drinking caffeinated beverages, George could try decaffeinated coffee and tea, or substitute another beverage for tea. Caffeine can make anxiety and agitation worse.

Other Possible Strategies to Consider

George might try working in his office in the morning when Ann is calmer. If he is able to focus on his work, he may have more patience for Ann because he is not worried about getting his office work done.

George might try one or more of these options to give Ann the attention she wants and give him the break he needs:

- He could hire a companion for Ann at that time of day. Ann's behavior is understandably stressful for both of them.

- George could ask a friend or neighbor to be with Ann.

- Ann might enjoy attending a day program where she could be with other people and participate in activities.

If all else fails, George should consult their doctor. If the level of agitation continues or increases, and puts both Ann and George at risk, it may be time to talk to her doctor about a medication to reduce the agitation and anger.

From George's behavior log, we were able to come up with a number of possible causes of Ann's behavior and strategies for responding to it. If keeping a log is not feasible for some reason, or if it doesn't yield clear results, find someone to help you systematically analyze the behavior. A friend, family member, or a health care professional may be able to assist with this. Your local Alzheimer's Association chapter may have someone available who can help.

If you brainstorm with someone else, often many possible causes emerge. Sometimes you can rule some of them out, but you may find that the list leads to a number of strategies to try.

When you sit down together, make a list of possible causes of the behavior. Think broadly. Perhaps it would help if you categorize causes. Below is an example:

Some possible physical or emotional causes of Ann's behavior:

- She's bored.
- She's lonely.
- She's hungry.
- She wants George's attention.
- She's craving sugar.
- She's had too much caffeine.
- She has to go to the bathroom.
- There's something she always did in the mid-afternoon that she is missing.

Possible causes related to the environment:

- The TV upset her.
- Something in George's office makes her uncomfortable.
- It's too hot or too cold.
- She can't find her way to the bathroom.

Finding some strategies that work to prevent or lessen the behavior can be extremely satisfying. Through detective work you will have lessened your relative's distress as well as your own. It is our hope that this handbook will give you an understanding of why common challenging behaviors occur and help you through the process of finding some possible solutions.

THE 4 A'S: ANXIETY, AGITATION, ANGER AND AGGRESSION

17

THE 4 A'S:
ANXIETY, AGITATION,
ANGER AND AGGRESSION

Christine Bryden, a woman with Alzheimer's disease, describes it like this:

"My stress tolerance is very low, and even a minor disruption can cause a catastrophic reaction, where I shout or scream, panic and pace. I need calm, no surprises, no sudden changes. Anxiety is an undercurrent in our disease. I feel I have to do something but can't remember what." (Bryden, p. 111)

Of all the behaviors associated with dementia, these behaviors are the ones that we hear about the most. They are also the ones that the media have often portrayed as characteristic of Alzheimer's disease. Every person is different – not everyone exhibits angry or aggressive behaviors, in fact it is a minority of people with dementia who do. Estimates about agitation vary widely but "nearly half of all people with dementia have agitation symptoms every month, including 30% of those living at home."(Livingston, et al., 2014, p.436) Agitated behaviors might include pacing, wringing one's hands, crying or making loud repetitive noises, trying to leave, or other behaviors that indicate distress.

Think about behavior as a form of communication. If you can figure out what your relative is trying to say with her agitation or anger, then you can figure out how to help her.

As people grow older, there appears to be an increase in anxiety among many. This is even more prevalent for those who develop dementia, although the anxiety may show up before the symptoms of dementia. It's easy to understand why your relative might feel anxious – imagine not being able to hold on to memories or keep track of what's happening, to have the world gradually become an unfamiliar, confusing and unpredictable place.

People with dementia most often become angry or combative (that is, start hitting or striking out) during personal care. This is understandable. None of us wants someone's help going to the toilet or taking a bath. It's personal and private and we have become independent in those areas as small children. To lose that independence is humiliating. (For specific suggestions related to personal care, see **Why Won't She Take a Bath?**, **When You Gotta Go**, and **Taking the Stress Out of Dressing**.)

While anxiety is quite different from anger, we believe that anxiety often leads to agitation, which may lead to anger and aggression. They are not the same but they can be related.

In **Becoming a Detective: A Problem-Solving Approach**, we have provided a case study of a woman who becomes very agitated. Reading this might help you understand possible causes and strategies for handling your relative's challenging behavior. There are often good reasons why people are agitated or angry and it is important to figure out what these reasons are so that you can prevent these behaviors. Think about behavior as a form of communication. If you can discover what your relative is trying to say with her agitation or anger, then you can figure out how to help her.

Possible Physical, Medical and Emotional Causes of Anxiety, Agitation, Anger and Aggression

- Whether brain changes from dementia directly cause agitation is not really understood, but is a possibility.

- Medication changes or side effects can increase anxiety and/or cause agitation.

- Physical illness can cause or increase agitation. Most people are anxious, agitated or irritable when ill and this is even more pronounced in people with dementia. Often this is called delirium, which is a rapid change in confusion level. If you see an overnight change in behavior, in level of disorientation or confusion, you should have your relative checked for delirium. (See **Glossary** for more information.)

- Untreated depression can cause anger. Untreated anxiety can cause agitation.

- The lifelong personality of the individual with dementia often has an impact on these behaviors. If your relative has always been an anxious person, it is likely that anxiety will increase with dementia. If she has been an angry person earlier in life, she may have more difficulty controlling her anger now. People who have needed to be in control of everything often have a particularly difficult time giving up control or allowing others to help.

- Pain can cause agitation. People with moderate or severe dementia may no longer be able to tell you that they are in pain. Their behavior may be the way they communicate discomfort.

- Sitting too long can cause physical discomfort that can lead to agitation or irritability.

- Fatigue can cause agitation and irritability in all of us. This is even more true in people with dementia. Tasks take more energy and anxiety can be exhausting.

- Needing to go to the bathroom can cause agitation. If your relative can't remember what to do or how to find the bathroom, it is likely she will become agitated.

- Feelings of uncertainty, frustration, fear, being trapped – all of these can lead to anxiety and agitation.

- Boredom can lead to agitation. When someone does not know what to do or how to fill time, it can cause anxiety or depression. Filling time becomes much more difficult for people with memory loss.

Strategies to Try for Possible Physical, Medical, and Emotional Causes of Anxiety, Agitation, Anger and Aggression

- Keeping a behavior log for a few days can be extremely helpful in understanding your relative's behavior. Refer to **Becoming a Detective: A Problem-Solving Approach** for ideas about how to do this. If you can identify patterns you can often get an idea of the cause and then figure out appropriate prevention strategies.

- If there is a fairly sudden change in behavior, arrange a medical evaluation to screen for infections or other physical causes of the behavior change. It may be delirium. Also have the doctor look carefully at medication changes or side effects that could be contributing to the problem.

- Request an evaluation for depression and anxiety. Medication for depression sometimes helps with angry behaviors. Some medications treat both depression and anxiety. If there are longstanding issues with anxiety or anger, discuss this with a mental health professional.

- Make sure pain is adequately treated. Arthritis, headaches or other chronic pain can cause irritability and agitation and is best treated on a regular schedule.

- Be sure your relative gets out of a chair or wheelchair and moves around on a regular basis. Think about how you feel when you sit for 4 or 5 hours without getting up. Older bodies are stiffer bodies. Regular stretching can be helpful.

- Make sure your relative gets enough rest throughout the day.

- Determine whether agitated behavior is related to the need to go to the bathroom.

> *Several times during the day, Hector Gonzàlez would pace from room to room, acting distressed and fumbling with his clothing. After keeping a log for a few days, his daughter, Bonita, finally realized that he did this when he needed to urinate. Walking with him to the bathroom as soon as she saw this behavior and switching his pants to elasticized waists almost eliminated the behavior.*

- As you become more skilled at observing your relative's behavior, try to figure out the feeling behind the behavior. Is she frightened? In pain? Anxious? Responding to the feeling is often one of the most helpful things you can do. *"Molly, you sound so frustrated. I am sorry you are having such a hard time with this."* While you are not solving the problem, Molly knows you are listening to her. *"Dad, you seem to be scared. Let's sit here together for a few minutes. I will be here to help you. You are not alone."*

- Try to find activities throughout the day that will engage your relative, even for a short time, to help alleviate boredom. This can be a difficult task for family members and will take some trial and error. Sometimes it is helpful, if possible, to find a companion to do things with her or to take her out. Adult day programs can also be a helpful remedy for people who are bored.

Possible Environmental Causes of Anxiety, Agitation, Anger and Aggression

- Sensory overload can make people agitated or angry. When an environment is too noisy, it can overload the person's ability to cope with it. Usually a person with dementia who is experiencing this will become angry, exhibit agitated behaviors or try to escape. Marie Linden would hold her head and moan when there were too many people in the room.

- Media such as television, radio or internet streaming may be too loud. A person with dementia may be overwhelmed by the noise. Also, at times people cannot sort out what is really happening versus what they are seeing or hearing on television. For some people the news, sirens, cop shows or other intense television may be frightening and lead to anxiety or agitation.

- Too much clutter can cause agitation; people with dementia may have difficulty sorting out what they are seeing. It is another kind of sensory overload which can be frustrating and overwhelming. We often see this during meals or in the bathroom, when there are too many things in front of the person and she is unable to pick out the item she needs or wants.

- An environment that is tense or angry is likely to prompt similar responses in a person with dementia. Despite dementia, individuals are often highly sensitive to the "emotional environment" at home or in a care setting and will quickly pick up on other people's tension or anxiety.

- Social situations with several people talking may be too overwhelming.

Strategies to Try for Possible Environmental Causes of Anxiety, Agitation, Anger and Aggression

- Help your relative leave an environment that is too crowded or noisy, or avoid the situation in the first place if you can. This might involve accompanying her to another room or turning off the noise. If your relative is in a residential care home this can be a more difficult problem to solve. If you observe her becoming agitated during meals or group activities, talk to staff about the possibility of a quiet space for residents like your relative.

- Try removing her from the television room. Or limit TV watching to soothing or calming programs.

Harold Black began to get very agitated during his favorite TV detective shows. His wife found that he responded better to old black and white movies that were popular during his youth. For several years he was happy watching them, but gradually he was unable to follow the plots and became agitated during them. She found a music streaming station that played old songs which Harold enjoyed. She also found sing-along DVDs to play for him. He began singing along with many of the songs and was often content for an hour at a time.

- Pay attention to the emotional environment in your home or your relative's care setting. Is the agitation a response to other people's moods, actions or tone of voice? If so, think about how you can create a calmer environment.

- Try to de-clutter the environment, especially areas where your relative does tasks (bathing, eating) or spends a lot of time. While you don't want to make the environment sterile, you do want to simplify it as needed.

- Avoid social situations with too many people if this agitates or upsets your relative. Although you may be trying to preserve social life and family gatherings, pay attention to whether these are becoming too much for your relative. Multiple, fast conversations start to be impossible for people with dementia to follow. Try smaller groups of family or friends instead of large gatherings.

"At other times I cannot follow what is going on around me; as the conversation whips too fast from person to person and before I have processed one comment, the thread has moved to another person or another topic, and I am left isolated from the action – alone in a crowd." (Davis, pp. 85-86)

Common Causes of Anger or Aggression

- As mentioned earlier, research indicates that most often anger and aggression occur during personal care such as bathing, going to the toilet, dressing. Frequently the person misunderstands the situation. She may feel threatened by someone trying to remove her clothes or touch her private areas, or feel humiliated, causing her to lash out.

- Feelings of frustration, loss of control and fear can lead to angry responses. People who had tempers earlier in life may have more trouble controlling their tempers now. When they feel threatened or that their privacy is invaded or when they are having trouble doing a task, they may be quick to anger.

- Feeling that one is being treated like a child, or that control is being taken away can lead to anger. Most of us like to be in control of our own lives but dementia gradually takes that control away. Even though it is the disease causing the problem, the anger is usually directed at the family member or caregiver.

- Being told "No."

- Poor communication by a caregiver can lead to angry responses.

Strategies to Try for Anger or Aggression

- Think about how to give your relative as much control as possible over decisions and situations that make her angry.

> *Robert Jones was furious with his wife for taking over the finances. Whenever money was mentioned, he shouted at her, accusing her of being a thief and a traitor. She learned ways of giving him back some of the control over finances. They began paying bills together. Even though Robert could not fill out the check anymore, he could still sign his name. She would hand him the bill and have him study it. It took a lot of patience on her part and much longer to pay the bills, but it avoided his anger because he believed he was in charge and she was just helping. Before they would go out to eat, she made sure Robert had cash in his wallet so that he could pay the bill. He often asked for help in making the right change, but again he felt that he was in charge.*

- Refer to other sections of this handbook for strategies related to personal care, if that is when your relative becomes angry.

Communication Strategies to Help Prevent Anxiety, Agitation, Anger and Aggression

The majority of angry responses probably occur because of poor communication. It is not easy to change our style of communicating with family members. It is hard not to be condescending or order someone around when we are overwhelmed or frustrated ourselves. But careful communication can make a huge difference. Some things to try:

- Make sure you explain step by step what you are doing during personal care or other tasks. *"Dad, I'm going to help you take your pants off now."*

- Give control and decision making to your relative as much as possible.

- Try not to say "No." Think of other ways to phrase things.

- Don't argue. You won't win and this frequently leads to anger.

- Think about your tone of voice. Do you sound patronizing or condescending? People with dementia are very quick to pick up on tone of voice and feel demeaned by it.

- Keep conversation simple but adult. Repeat slowly if your relative is having difficulty understanding.

- Acknowledge her feelings. *"Shelly, I can see that you are frustrated and angry."*

- Apologize if it will help. *"Mom, I am sorry this is so hard for you. If I am doing something to make it worse, I apologize."*

Staying Safe When Your Relative is Angry or Aggressive

It is important for you to be safe when your relative is out of control. Some things to think about or put in place include:

- Call for help. If you feel the situation is really out of control or you feel threatened, get help. This might be a neighbor or family member. Call 911 if you feel you are in danger.

- Stay calm. Don't raise your voice.

- Don't argue.

- Back off. Leave the room if need be. If you feel threatened, leave the house and go to a neighbor's.

- Don't get trapped. Keep yourself between your relative and the door so you can escape if you need to.

- If this is a frequent problem, talk with your relative's doctor.

Other Considerations for Anxiety, Agitation, Anger and Aggression

• Keep in mind that it is easier to prevent these types of behaviors than to defuse them once they have started. Using observation, behavior logs or whatever method helps you to understand possible causes of the behavior will help you to develop prevention strategies. Many of the other sections in this handbook describe behaviors that include agitation or anger. The prevention strategies there may be helpful in avoiding agitation during meals, bathing, going to the bathroom or when your relative is bored or upset.

• Probably the most useful thing you can do to prevent agitation in your relative, is to create a calm, consistent environment. Also find things for her to do that help alleviate boredom.

- It is not always possible to avoid anxiety or agitation. Sometimes it appears to be an inevitable part of the disease process. While medication is usually the last remedy to try, we recognize that sometimes it is necessary and helpful. However, there are potentially serious side effects to the psychiatric medications that are used to lessen agitation. Ask for help in weighing the pros and cons of medications.

References

Bryden, C. (2005). Dancing with Dementia. Jessica Kingsley Publishers.

Cohen-Mansfield, J., & Werner, P. (1995). Environmental influences on agitation: An integrative summary of an observational study. American Journal of Alzheimer's Disease and Other Dementias, 10(1), 32-39.

Davis, R. (1989). My Journey into Alzheimer's Disease. Tyndale House Publishers, Inc.

Livingston, G.; Kelly, L.; Lewis-Holmes, E.; Baio, G.; Morris, S.; Patel, N.; Omar, R.Z.; Katona, C. and Cooper, C. (2014). Non-Pharmacological Interventions for Agitation in Dementia: Systematic Review of Randomized Controlled Trials. The British Journal of Psychiatry, 205, 436-442.

Logsdon, R.G.; McCurry, S.M. and Teri, L (2007). Evidence-Based Psychological Treatments for Disruptive Behaviors in Individuals with Dementia. Psychology and Aging, 22(1), 28-36.

WHY WON'T SHE TAKE A BATH? HELPING YOUR RELATIVE WITH BATHING

WHY WON'T SHE TAKE A BATH?
HELPING YOUR RELATIVE WITH BATHING

Olivia Hernandez has lived with her daughter, Gabriela, for many years. She used to help around the house, babysitting, cooking, cleaning and gardening. In recent years Olivia has experienced some memory problems and confusion which have decreased her ability to help her daughter. About a year ago Gabriela noticed that her mother's hygiene was not as good as it used to be. As she paid more attention, Gabriela noticed that Olivia was not bathing for many days at a time. When she asked her mother about this, Olivia angrily denied it and said she was bathing every day. Gabriela had to work hard to figure out strategies for helping her mother bathe regularly without offending her sense of pride.

This is a common scenario in many families. Bathing is often the first personal care task that a person with dementia needs help with and it can be a very touchy and difficult issue. There are many possible causes of bathing challenges, but one of the most common is that people feel their privacy and dignity are being violated. We are all used to bathing ourselves, taking ourselves to the toilet and dressing ourselves. Research indicates that many of the aggressive, angry behaviors we see in people with dementia, occur in the context of personal care such as bathing.

Understanding that our family members often feel shame and a sense of violation when they need help with bathing is an important piece of solving bathing problems.

You might start approaching the bathing problem by asking yourself the kinds of questions that are listed in the **Becoming a Detective** section.

Possible Physical, Medical and Emotional Causes of Bathing Problems

- Brain changes from some forms of dementia can affect the bathing situation in a variety of ways:

  - Memory loss can cause people to lose track of when they have bathed. She may believe that she showered this morning when, in reality, it was several days ago.

  - Sequencing of tasks often becomes difficult in dementia. Bathing is a complex task made up of many steps. For some it may become too complicated and overwhelming.

- Pain from arthritis, neuropathy (nerve damage, see **Glossary**) or other causes may make bathing such a chore that it is avoided.

- Untreated depression can make it difficult for individuals to have the energy or desire to do anything that takes too much effort. For a frail older person, bathing can be strenuous.

- Fatigue, which often increases with dementia and can be a symptom of depression as well, makes it too difficult. Many people need to rest after bathing.

- Feeling one's privacy is being violated, as mentioned above, is often a primary cause of avoiding bathing.

- Fear of slipping or falling can cause individuals to avoid bathing. Many older people know that bathrooms are a common site of accidents, broken hips, etc. If balance is an issue or the bathroom is not well adapted (see below – **Environmental Strategies**), this may be a possible reason your relative avoids bathing.

- Water may not feel good on your relative's skin any more. Sometimes because of changes in the brain, people experience the sensation of water differently. Their sense of temperature may have changed. Or sometimes people will say the water is painful on their skin or feels like "bugs crawling" or "pins and needles." Clearly if the sensation of water is unpleasant people will avoid it.

- In later stages of dementia, it is not uncommon for people to feel frightened of having water come over their heads and faces.

Strategies to Try for Possible Physical, Medical and Emotional Causes of Bathing Problems

- If problems start suddenly, always suspect an infection or another medical cause and take your relative to her doctor.

- Have your relative evaluated for pain or depression if you suspect these causes. Sometimes an aspirin or anti-inflammatory prior to bathing can be very helpful, but check first with your relative's physician.

- When memory loss is the cause, you might try a bathing chart with dates on it or marking a calendar. Some people respond well to this; it makes others angry.

- If your relative becomes confused or overwhelmed, simplify the task of bathing for her. This might involve setting up the bathroom, getting the water the right temperature, helping with undressing. She might be able to bathe herself with just a little assistance.

- Think about the time of day. While you want to try to follow your relative's prior bathing habits and schedule, you also want to pay attention to fatigue levels. If she's always bathed at night but is now exhausted or more confused by early evening you might try a different time of day.

- Ask your relative why she doesn't like to bathe. She may be able to tell you the reason herself, especially if it is fear, pain or privacy issues.

- When privacy is the primary issue, try some of the strategies listed in **Ensuring Comfort and Privacy**, later in this section.

- When the water doesn't feel right, try some of the strategies listed in **Ensuring Comfort and Privacy**.

- Separating hair washing from bathing may help with the fear and discomfort of having water on the head. Some care partners arrange for beauty parlor visits for hair washing or try using a dry shampoo.

- Give her a washcloth to hold over her face during hair washing.

- A shampoo tray that allows you to wash your relative's hair while she sits in a chair may help her feel more comfortable and less fearful of getting wet.

Possible Environmental Causes of Bathing Problems

Jack Spangler stopped bathing as his dementia progressed. Rachel, his wife, asked him to shower with her one morning to see if she could understand it. Jack was very hesitant. As he tried to climb over the tub to get in, she realized that he was shivering, that there was nothing for him to hold onto, and that he was very frightened. She was able to work with a local social service agency to have grab bars and a hand held shower installed and to purchase a shower chair. She bought a heater to warm the bathroom ahead of time and made sure she was in the room to reassure Jack when he showered.

- The bathroom may not feel safe.

- The bathroom may be too cold or the room too drafty.

- The lighting may be poor, making the room frightening or causing hallucinations.

- The water temperature fluctuates causing unexpected cold or hot spells.

- The bath or shower controls may be unfamiliar and difficult for her to operate.

- There may be too much clutter, distracting your relative from focusing on bathing.

- There may not be enough color contrast between the bathing area and bathing supplies. For example, a white bathtub, white washcloth and white bar of soap may all blend in together, making it difficult for your relative to locate the washcloth and soap.

Bathing is often the first personal care task that a person with dementia needs help with and it can be a very touchy and difficult issue.

Strategies to Try for Possible Environmental Causes of Bathing Problems

- Evaluate the bathroom for needed adaptations for safety or ease getting in and out. See websites at the end of this chapter for home modification information. Common adaptations include:

  – Grab bars

  – Hand held showers, which can give the person more control

  – Shower or bath chairs or bath transfer benches

  – Installing a walk-in shower

- Try heating up the bathroom ahead of time.

- Improve the lighting if it is dim. Sometimes it is dark behind shower curtains, which scares people.

- De-clutter the bathroom if that is an issue, especially if your relative becomes confused or distracted during the bathing process.

Safety Strategies in the Bathroom

- Adjust the temperature setting on the water heater to no more than 120 degrees.

- Use non-slip, washable bathmats inside and outside of the tub or shower.

- Make sure the floor of the tub or shower is non-slip material or has a bathmat. Test it yourself to see if it is slippery with soapsuds on it.

- Do not leave your relative alone while she is bathing in the later stages of illness.

- Don't use breakable glass containers in the bathroom.

Possible Communication Challenges Related to Bathing Problems

- Communication is often a large factor when a person is reluctant to bathe. Without meaning to, care partners often sound bossy, especially when they are tired or frustrated and just want their relative to take a bath. This tends to breed resentment and resistance to being told what to do.

- Caregivers may not be explaining things clearly enough or giving step by step instructions. If your relative does not understand what's going on, it may increase her fear or anxiety.

Ensuring Comfort and Privacy

Joan McCay hated having anyone assist her with bathing and became quite angry whenever it was attempted. Her daughter, Alice, began to think about the whole bathing experience from "setting the stage" for a bath to sharing a pleasant experience with her mother after the bath was finished. She decided to try a new approach. First, Alice got the bathroom ready and turned on the heater. Then she and her mother looked at a favorite photo album together. Next Alice said, "Mom, the shower is ready. Let me help you off with your shirt and give you a hand into the shower so you don't slip." Joan started to get angry and Alice replied, "Mom, John is coming to visit later and I know you want to look nice. I'll help you." After she had her mom seated in the shower, Alice used the hand held sprayer to help her get the water the right temperature. Then she put a towel around her shoulders, gave her mother the washcloth and had her wash while Alice held the sprayer the way her mother wanted it. When Joan was dressed again, Alice had a snack waiting for her. Although there were some tense moments, the bathing process went much more smoothly than in the past. Alice practiced remaining calm and ignoring angry outbursts.

- Try to make the bathroom as comfortable, warm and inviting as possible.

- Think about how you are going to approach this conversation ahead of time if your relative resists bathing. What can you use as a hook or reward? Alice used John's upcoming visit. Some caregivers have used an upcoming trip to church , synagogue or mosque. Others have used a dish of ice cream or a treat as a reward at the end of the bath or shower.

- Try to give the person as much control as possible – over the decision and over the process. Instead of asking, *"Would you like to take your bath now?"* Try asking, *"Would you like your bath now, before you get dressed, or tonight before bed?"* This gives the person a feeling of more control.

- Sometimes it's better to be direct and simple. *"Harold, your bath is ready."*

- Try to mimic previous routines as much as possible to make it feel familiar. Ask about the preferred soap, hair washing method, etc. All of us have routines that we rely on and it can be uncomfortable when these are changed, especially if someone is switching from a bath to a shower, from morning to night, or some other large change in routine.

- Try as much as possible to schedule bathing at the same time she is used to.

- Try to schedule the bath or shower in the morning or at night so there is not unnecessary dressing and redressing in the middle of the day, as this can be tiring and confusing.

- Music can help create a calming environment. If there is a type of soft music that your relative enjoys, you might try playing it throughout the bathing process.

- If your relative particularly dislikes receiving help from a family member, consider hiring a home health aide to assist with bathing. If you do, you might want to have the aide help with other things as well, such as changing beds or laundry. You might not want to introduce bathing until your relative has established a relationship with the aide.

- Encourage your relative to test the temperature of the water before getting into the tub or shower. Continue to ask about the temperature throughout the process.

- Drape a towel over your relative's shoulders or lap if privacy is an issue. Some families have had the person shower in her underwear or bathing suit to protect modesty.

- Warm a towel in the dryer ahead of time if your relative tends to get cold.

- Monitor your relative's skin for sores or skin breakdown, especially if incontinence is an issue or if she is sitting most of the time.

- Check your relative's feet for skin sores, dry skin, ingrown nails or nails that need trimming.

- If your relative is frightened by the water needed to wash her hair, try wetting her head with washcloths, baby shampoo, rinsing with a small amount of water, and deflecting water from face and ears.

- Give her a washcloth to hold over her face so the water does not go into her eyes or mouth.

- Try a bed bath for a person who is in the late stages of dementia, is very frail, has very limited mobility, or is very frightened and agitated when bathing. Again, a home health aide could be very helpful with this.

- No matter how much sensitivity and care is put into the bathing process, there are times when it can be a considerable challenge.

References and Resources

Web sites for general information on home modifications and products including bathrooms:

www.infinitec.org/live/homemodifications/bathrooms.htm

www.eldercare.gov/Eldercare.NET/Public/Resources/Factsheets/Home_Modifications.aspx

www.makoa.org

www.abledata.com (Go to products, then environmental adaptations, then bathrooms.)

TAKING THE
STRESS
OUT OF
DRESSING

TAKING THE STRESS
OUT OF DRESSING

Getting dressed is a very personal and private activity. When people start to have difficulty with it, they often feel frustrated and embarrassed and are reluctant to accept help. The loss of independence can be terribly difficult for some people with dementia.

For those of us without dementia, it is hard to imagine why or how one could have difficulty with it. We dress ourselves daily without giving it any thought. But dressing is actually more complex than we might think, often making it challenging for people in the middle or later stages of dementia. Dressing involves a number of steps and abilities: making a decision about what to wear; selecting specific articles of clothing; remembering the order of each step of getting dressed and coordinating our limbs with the clothing.

A generation ago many people did not change their clothes as often as we do today. It is important not to impose our values about how often we think others need to change clothes.

Possible Physical, Medical and Emotional Causes of Dressing and Undressing

- Physical changes in the brain can result in:

  - Memory loss. A person with dementia may forget how to dress or undress, or if she is getting dressed or undressed. Or she may have forgotten the last time she changed her clothes.

  - Shortened attention span. The task of getting dressed exceeds the person's attention span.

  - The inability to identify items of clothing, for example, confusing a jacket and a sweater.

  - The inability to recognize or coordinate parts of the body. The partial or total loss of recognizing objects or items is known as agnosia.

  - The inability to sequence the steps of getting dressed in the right order, such as what to put on first, second, etc.

  - No longer being able to make decisions about what to wear.

  - Impaired judgment. Some people may no longer know what is appropriate clothing for weather conditions or social events.

- Depression can cause a person with dementia to lose interest in getting dressed or looking good.

- Physical illnesses can cause a lack of interest in her appearance.

- Pain, such as arthritis, can affect range of motion in arms and hands. Hip and knee pain may limit a person's ability to stand or put a foot in a pant leg.

- Impaired vision may prevent a person from seeing that clothes are soiled.

- Changes in fine motor coordination skills may make it difficult to manage buttons and zippers.

- Changes in gross motor skills can affect balance and may cause a person to fear falling.

- Side effects of some medications may cause dizziness or stiff joints.

- She may feel too tired to get dressed or undressed.

- The person feels embarrassed about getting dressed or undressed in front of another person.

- Accepting help getting dressed makes her feel a loss of control.

- She may feel humiliated that she is being reminded to get dressed or change her clothes.

- The person with dementia feels anxious because she may not recognize the caregiver.

Strategies to Try for Possible Physical, Medical and Emotional Causes of Dressing and Undressing

- Keep a diary or log in order to pinpoint whether there are particular times of the day when your relative may be more interested and involved in getting dressed or undressed. Your relative may be more able and willing to change clothes when she is more rested.

- Schedule an appointment with the doctor to discuss possible causes such as side effects of medications, depression or physical conditions that may be causing imbalance, pain or stiffness.

- Schedule an eye exam to determine if vision has changed or if new conditions are present. Cataracts, glaucoma, macular degeneration, as well as normal vision changes with aging, can affect balance, depth perception and a comfort level and ability to get dressed.

Dressing is actually more complex than you might think.

- If balance is a problem, your relative may feel more comfortable sitting in a chair or having a chair nearby for support while getting dressed or undressed.

- Let your relative get dressed on her own for as long as she can. Being able to dress oneself, even partially, gives a person a sense of control, accomplishment, and independence.

- Be sure that she knows who you are. *"Mom, I'm going to help you get dressed now."* Or *"Dorothy, I'm your husband. It's ok for me to help you get dressed."*

Clothing Considerations

- Select clothing that fits comfortably. Stiffness and muscle tension can make dressing very difficult for some people. Purchasing clothes that are one size larger may make it easier to get clothes on and off.

- Try garments with front closures. Shirts, dresses, pajamas and cardigan sweaters that button all the way down the front may be less painful to get on and off for people affected by arthritis or mobility problems. Seeing front closures may also help your relative participate in getting dressed.

- Make sure all closures are undone before starting: buttons are unbuttoned, zippers are unzipped, snaps are unsnapped, etc.

- For some people, buttons, snaps, zippers and belt buckles are too difficult to manage. Replace them with Velcro® closures.

- Active style clothing - sweat pants and jackets that zip down the front - are easy to get on and off, are warm and are easy to launder.

- Choose footwear that is comfortable, easy to get on and off, has a skid proof sole and offers adequate support. If edema (swelling in the feet or ankles) is an issue, regularly evaluate if shoes are the right length and width. Shoes with Velcro® closures can be easily adapted for swelling in the feet and ankles.

When Buying New Clothes

- Choose clothes that reflect the person's taste as much as possible. Consider the person's preferred styles and colors.

- Choose clothes with simple patterns. Bright, busy patterns can be distracting. Also, select solid contrasting colors. These tend to be easier for older people to distinguish.

- If your relative wants to wear the same clothing every day, consider purchasing several identical outfits. This will allow you to replace soiled clothing with clean clothes.

> *Mary would only wear a certain pair of black pants and a black sweater. Her son tried to talk to her about changing her soiled clothes, but Mary did not see the food stains and was insulted that her son said she was wearing dirty clothes. Sam purchased several identical new black outfits for his mom that were similar to the ones she liked so much. After Mary was asleep, Sam removed the soiled clothing, removed the sales tag from the new outfits, and put them in Mary's room. The next morning Mary dressed herself without commenting on her new pants and sweater.*

- Consider buying "adaptive clothing." These clothing items have been adapted for easier dressing but often have the appearance of a normal garment. There are many resources for adaptive clothing online and in some retail stores.

  - Hidden but accessible Velcro® closures on the inside of a shirt can be fastened. Buttons on the outside give the appearance of a "normal" garment.

  - Pants that have zippers on the legs may make it easier to get the pants on and off.

  - Blouses and shirts with closures in the back may make it easier to change clothing when a person is in a wheelchair.

Clothing for Women

- For women who have a hard time putting on a bra, try one with a closure in the front. For some women, a camisole, t-shirt or vest may be more comfortable than a bra; however, many women have worn a bra all their adult life and will be uncomfortable not wearing one.

- Purchase loose fitting underwear.

- Avoid slips unless she feels uncomfortable without them.

- Avoid knee-high stockings as they often are too tight but may not feel tight to women with dementia. Knee-highs are not good for people with circulation problems.

- Shoe peds or shoe liners can be worn with shoes or slippers and provide skin protection. Some styles have a cushioned pad that provides added comfort on the bottom of the foot.

- There are many colorful styles of socks available that not only provide warmth but can also be fun to wear.

- Elastic waistbands on skirts and pants may be more comfortable, and easier to get on and off when your relative needs to go to the bathroom.

- Wrap around skirts can be put on while sitting and may be easier to manage for women in wheelchairs or who find it difficult to stand while getting dressed.

Clothing for Men

- Try using suspenders or pants with elastic waistbands.

> *Robert was having some episodes of incontinence, in part because it was taking him longer to undo his belt, unbutton and unzip his pants. His wife, Mary, suggested he wear some sweat pants "to see if they are more comfortable for you." Mary felt Robert was agreeable because she talked about making him comfortable and not about his incontinence.*

- Avoid belts if buckling and unbuckling a belt becomes too frustrating, painful or takes too long to fasten or unfasten.

- Tube socks are easier to get on and off because they do not have heels. Most elastic bands at the top of the sock will leave a slight mark, but if there is a deeper indentation, it usually indicates the socks are too tight.

- Consider buying T-shirts. They tend to look okay even if worn backwards.

Possible Environmental Causes of Dressing Challenges

- The room temperature is too hot or cold.

- The dressing area lacks privacy.

- Poor lighting – the person is unable to see clothes in the closet or the drawers.

- Too many distractions can affect a person's ability to focus on the task of dressing (or undressing), such as too many people in the room, too much clutter or noise.

- Closet or drawers contain too many garments, making it difficult for the person to clearly see articles of clothing and to make a choice of what to wear.

- Clothing is not well organized. Having winter and summer clothing or dressy and everyday clothing mixed together makes it more difficult for a person with dementia to choose appropriate clothes.

- She may not be able to remember what is behind a closet door or in a closed drawer.

Strategies to Try for Possible Environmental Causes of Dressing Challenges

- Make sure that the room is warm enough for your relative. Remember that some older adults, and especially those with dementia, may need a warmer room to feel comfortable. A caregiver may feel it is oppressively hot inside the house while the person with dementia finds the temperature comfortable. Clothing with long sleeves can keep the person warm and also protect fragile skin.

- Create a sense of privacy by closing the door, blinds and curtains.

- Avoid times when other people might interrupt and disturb your relative while she is getting dressed. If other people are present, post a "Do Not Disturb" sign on the door to let others know not to interrupt.

- Door or drawer pulls rather than knobs may provide easier access to closets and drawers, especially when a person has arthritis.

- Provide adequate lighting in the bedroom. Make sure overhead lights and table lamps are not casting shadows that could be distracting or misinterpreted. A light in the closet may help the person to see and select clothing.

- Turn off cell phones or other electronic devices that could be distracting and disrupt getting dressed.

- Try dressing in a room where your relative has always dressed or undressed. This might be the bedroom, bathroom or another private space. If your relative requires your assistance, make sure the dressing area is large enough for her and you to move comfortably and safely. Dressing in the bathroom may provide privacy but may not allow adequate space for both of you.

- Keep the room free of clutter. People with dementia can be easily distracted by clutter or the appearance that things need to be straightened.

- Simplify the decision of what to wear by limiting the number of clothing items in drawers and closets. Remove rarely worn clothes and out of season clothes.

- Label dresser drawers describing the contents (shirts, underwear, socks). Some people are more accepting of labels if they are involved in sticking on decorative labels.

- Assemble all articles of clothing and accessories that are to be worn together. Hang pants or skirt with matching shirt, sweater, underwear, and any other accessories on one hanger.

- Layer clothes on a bed in the order in which they will be put on. Put undergarments on top of the pile. The second article of clothing (blouse, shirt, skirt) is next, etc. Make sure all articles of clothing are right side out. Arranging clothes on a bedspread or blanket of a contrasting color may help a person to see the articles of clothing better.

- Try putting socks inside of the shoes.

- If your relative is able to choose what to wear, give her two choices. If she is not able to make a choice, have garments ready and within reach.

Other Possible Causes of Dressing Challenges

- Your relative feels rushed or is still sleepy.

- The caregiver is not giving simple or clear enough directions causing the person with dementia to feel confused about what she is expected to do.

- The person with dementia misinterprets the caregiver's actions, causing her to feel scared and anxious.

- She associates certain clothing with behaviors: when she wears pajamas she feels she needs to go to bed; when wearing dressy clothes, she may expect to go to church or to work.

Dick was a policeman for 40 years. He was proud to walk his 'beat' in his uniform, watching for people who needed help and those who had committed crimes. After he developed Alzheimer's disease, he continued to wear his heavy uniform jacket while he walked, often getting overheated. Rather than try to stop Dick from walking, Marge pinned his badges on a lighter jacket and told him, "Sargent said uniforms have changed for the police force and sent you this new jacket. "

Strategies to Try for Other Possible Causes of Dressing Challenges

- Try to follow your relative's dressing routine as much as possible. Consider how the person started her day in the past. What was her morning routine? Did she have breakfast before or after getting dressed?

- Lay clothes out ahead of time if decisions are difficult. This can help promote independence and feelings of control.

- Try not to awaken your relative to get dressed. If she does not like to be awakened, she may start her day grumpy or angry. Also, she may not be able to fully participate in getting dressed.

- Spend some time talking or doing something with your relative before getting dressed. This helps some people relax and feel more comfortable changing clothes.

- Schedule plenty of time for your relative to do as much as she can for herself and not feel rushed. Keep in mind that it can take longer than you think for your relative to process what you are asking her to do and then do it.

- When caregivers feel rushed, there can be an unintentional result of dressing the person, creating a premature dependency on the caregiver. Involving her in dressing can help her feel successful and accomplished.

- Music may help relax your relative. Try playing familiar and favorite music before or during dressing. Encourage her to sing along.

- Engaging her in conversation throughout the dressing process may help her relax. Keep in mind some people may need quiet while getting dressed to help them focus on instructions and manage the sequence of steps.

- Give your relative a reason to get dressed. *"Mom, we are going out for lunch today with Jane. I know she loves to see you in this yellow blouse and your gray pants."*

- If the person with dementia refuses to change clothes, it may be easier to try again later.

- Offer your relative assistance, but if she refuses your help, stand by, ready to help when asked.

> *Jean's mom had always been a very private and independent person and these personality traits did not change when she was diagnosed with dementia. Although her mom had difficulty getting dressed, she refused Jean's help, saying, "I can do this this by myself." Rather than argue, Jean would say, "OK, mom, let me know if you need some help. I will wait right outside the door." After a few minutes, Jean's mom would call to Jean, "OK, I guess I need some help now."*

Possible Causes for Undressing in Public Areas

It can be embarrassing for a caregiver when a relative takes her clothes off in public. This behavior is a reflection of the disease process and not of the person's morality. Sometimes the part of the brain that helps us recognize what is appropriate to do or wear in public has been damaged. A good place to start is to ask yourself some questions that might explain why your relative is undressing.

- Is the person too warm?

- Is she uncomfortable?

- Is the clothing too heavy, twisted, or scratchy?

- Does she not like the style or color of clothing that she is wearing?

- Does she need to go to the bathroom?

- Was she incontinent and wants to change her clothes?

- Is she tired and trying to get ready for bed?

- Does she want to take a bath?

Strategies to Try for Disrobing

- Review the questions above. Your relative may not be able to tell you with her words how she is feeling, but her behavior may be telling you what she needs.

- Try to determine if disrobing occurs approximately the same time of day. This may indicate your relative is ready for bed or needs to go to the bathroom.

- Investigate if there is something in the clothing that is making her uncomfortable: scratchy threads, tags, binding cuffs or waistband, tight collar, etc.

- Slide the belt buckle to the back of the pants.

- Try jumpsuits or one piece outfits that zip up the back. Keep in mind that this may help with disrobing but be a challenge for toileting.

- Try to be respectful in correcting the problem. Remember that this is not intentional misbehavior.

> *When Sally's dad began undressing in public, Sally would escort her dad to a more private area and say, "Dad, let's go over here so I can help you with that." She also had a card printed that explained to onlookers why her dad was acting this way. "My dad is doing the best he can. He has Alzheimer's disease."*

Possible Causes For Layering or Wearing Clothes Inside Out or Backwards

Some people develop a habit of putting on multiple layers of clothing, regardless of the weather. Some also put on clothes in random order. For example, a woman might put on a dress, then her slip, followed by two sweaters.

Again, asking some questions about the behavior can be helpful.

- Is the person cold?

- Is she fearful of losing her clothes or someone stealing them?

- Does she have access to too many clothes in her closet or drawers?

- Has she forgotten that she is already fully dressed?

- Has she forgotten what to put on first, second, etc.?

- Is she bored and looking for something to do?

- Has she forgotten how to dress?

- Is she unable to distinguish front from back, inside from outside?

- Is she trying to hide the dirty side of the clothes?

- Is she unable to focus on what she is doing due to shortened attention span?

Strategies to Try When Clothes are Layered or Worn Inside Out or Backwards

- Check your relative's skin temperature to make sure she is not cold.

- Don't do anything. Is there any reason why the person should not wear the extra clothing? Is it harmful, e.g., putting her at risk for getting overheated? If wearing extra clothing is not causing harm, it may be better to accept what your relative is wearing.

- Limit access to clothing in closets and drawers.

- Lay out the clothes for the day and keep other clothing out of sight.

- Lay clothes right side up on bed.

- Choose clothing where the front and back look similar, such as t-shirts. Your relative will not have to make a decision about what is the front and back.

- Stick a removable note on front of garment that says, *"This is the front of your shirt."*

- Place a decorative pin or label on the front of the shirt, being cautious about any harm this might present.

- Try to be flexible and accepting that your relative is doing the best she can to get dressed.

Communication Tips for Dressing Challenges

- Approach the person from the front. Introduce yourself if she doesn't always remember you. Explain that you are there to help her get dressed (or undressed). Maintain eye contact. *"Mom, it's Jennifer and I am here to help you get dressed. Is this a good time?"*

- Give your relative time to acknowledge your presence before you begin the dressing process.

- Give your relative a choice of what she wants to wear. Show her the choice of garments. Use the name of the clothing item: *"Would you like to wear this blue shirt or this red shirt?"*

- Begin by complimenting your relative: *"Mildred, your hair looks great today. I will try very hard not to mess it up."* or *"This color of blue is your color, Mildred. It matches your eyes."*

- Hand her one item at a time. Describe what you are handing her: *"Mom, here is your pink blouse."*

- Encourage your relative to participate as much as she can during the dressing process. *"Jane, can you put your arm in this sleeve?"*

- Offer praise and thanks for her participation and help. *"Thank you Sally for helping me with that snap. I really appreciate your help."*

- Give your relative enough time to start or finish the steps before offering assistance.

- Ask your relative if she needs help. Watch for signs of frustration. If she appears frustrated, casually offer help, *"Mom, I know this might be hard for you. Let me help you."*

- Although the problem may be cognitive, sometimes blaming it on physical limitations is more acceptable. *"I know your shoulder doesn't work very well. Can I help you get that top on?"*

EATING: THE INGREDIENTS FOR SUCCESSFUL MEALS

EATING:
THE INGREDIENTS FOR SUCCESSFUL MEALS

When we are hungry, we eat. We know what we like and don't like to eat. We have our routines and habits that often have developed over a lifetime and we continue to include mealtime rituals without giving it much thought.

Adapting the dining experience is often necessary to reduce stress and frustration for the person with dementia and the care partner. This section offers some common causes for eating challenges and suggestions for how to make mealtimes more successful for you and your relative.

Possible Physical, Medical and Emotional Causes of Eating Challenges

Physical changes in the brain can affect eating habits, including overeating or undereating.

Overeating

- A person may forget that she has recently eaten and wants to eat shortly after finishing a meal.

- She may experience a constant sensation of being hungry despite eating regular meals. This may be a result of misinterpreting the sensations in her stomach.

- An increased craving for sweets may occur. The person with dementia may have an appetite for sweets and prefer foods with high sugar content such as ice cream, bananas, candy, cookies, etc. This is particularly common in people with Frontotemporal Dementia (FTD) but also often occurs in the middle stages of Alzheimer's disease.

Undereating

- Your relative may experience a sensation of being full even though she has not eaten.

- She may have lost the ability to recognize hunger or thirst.

- She may no longer be able to verbally express hunger and thirst or food likes and dislikes.

- It may be difficult for her to get started, or initiate the task of eating on her own.

- Your relative may no longer remember how to use eating utensils.

- She may no longer remember how to chew food.

- A shortened attention span or the need to move can make it difficult for a person to sit at the table for an entire meal.

- The ability to recognize food as food, and as something to eat is sometimes lost (agnosia).

- She may have difficulty closing her lips around the spoon due to changes in the brain.

- Only a portion of the plate can be seen due to "one side neglect." This is particularly common after strokes. The person's visual field has been affected and she can only see part of what is in front of her.

- In the later stages, eating may become less enjoyable due to discomfort when swallowing or the fear of choking.

- Eating alone can diminish appetite as eating is often a social activity.

Strategies to Try for Overeating or Eating Too Much

- Try to determine how much of the meal your relative is eating, especially if she is asking for food shortly after meals. If she is eating all of her food, serving larger portions may help decrease requests for snacks in between meals.

- If she continues to want additional snacks after eating, and weight gain is a concern, try serving smaller meals and offer small snacks upon request. High protein snacks such as peanut butter, yogurt, cheeses, etc., may satisfy her appetite longer.

- Try increasing the number of meals to 5 or 6, if possible.

- Leaving healthy low calorie snacks such as fruit and vegetables on the table or counter may be enough to satisfy your relative.

- Try limiting sweets or offering smaller portions. Offer dessert after the meal is finished. Limit access to cookies, candy and other sweets. Offer sweets as a special treat. Try negotiation: *"Ethel, let's both have our cake at the end of the meal."*

- Offer low calorie substitutes such as nonfat or low fat ice cream, or yogurt.

- Ask your doctor if any medications could be causing an increased desire for sweets. Some anti-depressants can cause cravings for sweet foods.

- Monitor her weight. The shape of her body may be changing but there may not actually be weight gain.

- Many people who move into residential care homes gain weight for many reasons: they might not have been eating 3 meals a day or eating nutritious food before the move; portions are also often larger and contain more calories than the person had previously been eating.

- Increase exercise. Consider if your relative is getting enough exercise to offset the increased amount of food she is eating. Taking daily walks may help.

- Try increasing social contacts and activities. Some people with dementia eat out of boredom and do not know how else to satisfy themselves.

Strategies to Try for Undereating or Eating Too Little

- Offer favorite snacks throughout the day. Add dietary supplements such as Ensure® that provide added calories and nutrients.

- Observe if your relative is eating food from all areas on the plate. If your relative is eating from only one side of the plate – either the right or left side – it could mean that she does not see the whole plate and is only eating what she sees. When she has eaten food on one side of the plate, try rotating the plate, so the remaining food is in her field of vision.

- Serve smaller portions. Large meals can be confusing, distracting and unappealing for people with dementia. A common comment from people with dementia when they are served a large meal is *"I can't possibly eat all of that."* They often push their plate away when it feels overwhelming.

- Present the meal "ready to eat" as soon as the person arrives at the table, if your relative is anxious about sitting and eating. Have food cut in bite size pieces, beverage poured, and needed eating utensils accessible and in sight.

- Offer your relative food that she can eat while she walks if she is unable to sit through a meal. Finger foods such as fruit slices, chicken bites, and vegetables can be eaten on the go. Be cautious of choking hazards with all foods at all times.

- Serve one course of the meal at a time if your relative has difficulty sitting through the whole meal, e.g., serve soup first and then a sandwich. The decision of how long to wait between courses varies from person to person and may vary from day to day.

- Show her the utensil she will be using to eat. *"Rosa, this is the spoon for your soup. Let me put it in your hand."*

- Help your relative get started. With your hand on hers, help her locate the food on her plate, tell her what she is eating and then assist her with moving the food to her mouth. She may require assistance at the beginning of the meal and be able to continue on her own for the remainder of the meal or require periodic assistance.

- Ask the doctor about medications: Could a prescription or an over-the counter medication be causing drowsiness that interferes with finishing her meals? If so, can the medication be given at another time? Could one or more of her medications be suppressing her appetite?

- Putting on upbeat music or involving her in a conversation during mealtime may help keep her awake without overstimulating her.

- Try to make sure someone sits with your relative and eats with her.

- Check your relative's weight regularly to determine if weight loss has occurred.

Additional Physical, Medical and Emotional Causes of Eating Challenges

- Age related sensory changes can affect a person's interest in eating. A diminished sense of smell and taste can make food less appealing. Vision changes may affect the person's ability to see and manage getting the food from the table to her mouth.

- Sore gums, loose or ill fitting dentures, tooth decay or pain and dry mouth can make chewing uncomfortable or painful. (See Section on **Mouth Care**.)

- Pain caused by arthritis can make it difficult to hold a fork, mug or glass.

- Physical discomfort, caused by numerous conditions including constipation, arthritis, back and knee pain, etc., may cause a decrease in appetite.

- Your relative could be incontinent and is uncomfortable sitting in wet clothing.

- Fatigue can cause her to fall asleep during a meal and she may be unable to finish eating.

- Depression can affect your relative's desire to eat. A person who is depressed may lose interest in eating. Conversely, a person affected by depression can have an increased appetite.

- Dehydration can cause increases in confusion and susceptibility to urinary tract infections, both of which can affect appetite.

- Swallowing may become difficult in later stages of dementia for some people.

Strategies for Responding to Additional Physical, Medical and Emotional Causes of Eating Challenges

- Make sure your relative is wearing her glasses and can see the food.

- Encourage your relative to take a rest before meals if she is falling asleep during meals.

- Schedule an appointment with the dentist to check for gum sores, tooth decay, and broken or ill fitting dentures. (See Section on **Mouth Care**.)

- Schedule a thorough medical evaluation with your relative's doctor to rule out possible causes of acute changes in eating habits, including infection, constipation, illness, dehydration, pain, and untreated or undertreated anxiety and depression.

- Take your relative to the toilet before mealtime if possible. Needing to go to the bathroom during mealtime can lead to restlessness and not being able to focus on eating.

- Moistening food with sauces, gravies and other liquids may help with dry mouth.

- Discuss the need for soft foods with the doctor if your relative is having chewing problems. Soft foods such as eggs, creamed soups, cottage cheese, gelatins, etc. can be easier to chew and swallow.

- Consult with the doctor about a referral to a speech therapist or a dietician who can help make swallowing easier and prevent choking. Pureed foods can also be used if all else fails. One of these professionals can also assist you in making pureed foods more attractive, nutritious and flavorful.

- Try large handle utensils if holding a spoon or fork is painful. Slide a soft hair roller on the utensil handle or purchase adapted utensils from a pharmacy or medical supply company.

- Try finger foods if your relative has trouble holding a fork or spoon, or is confused about how to use a utensil.

> *Rozena watched her husband, Joe, try to eat his dinner: a salad, meat, diced potatoes and green beans. He took his spoon and tried to eat the meat but that didn't work. He tried using the handle of the spoon to dish up the potatoes, but that didn't work either. Finally, Joe put the spoon down and used his fingers. He finished his dinner successfully on his own. From that point on, Rozena served Joe finger foods that he could manage.*

- To avoid dehydration, offer water and non-caffeinated beverages throughout the day. Make sure the beverage is within sight and reach. This provides a visual cue for your relative to drink. Provide a verbal reminder when necessary, *"Mom, your water is right beside you. Please take a drink of it."*

Possible Environmental Causes of Eating Challenges

- Your relative could be distracted or stressed by other people's movements and conversations, sounds from appliances such as the dishwasher, TV, radio or outdoor noises.

- The temperature of the dining room may be too hot or too cold. Drafty areas or "hotspots" in the dining area may be uncomfortable.

- Inadequate lighting can make it difficult to see and distinguish the food from other items on the table.

- Glare from lighting or windows can be distracting or cause a person to be anxious.

- The dining chair could be uncomfortable: too small, too hard, not the right height for the table, etc.

- The table may be cluttered with too many dishes and utensils, condiments, decorations, etc.

- Busy patterned table linens or patterned plates – ones with bright colors, floral prints, geometric designs – can be distracting and make it difficult for a person with dementia to locate the plate and food.

- A lack of contrast between the plate and table linens can also make it challenging for people with spatial impairment.

- It can be difficult to distinguish food from the plate, especially when the food and the plate are similar in color, e.g., chicken, potatoes, cauliflower or applesauce on a white plate.

Strategies for Responding to Possible Environmental Causes of Eating Challenges

- Minimize all distractions. Keep conversations to a minimum. Answer phone calls away from the dining area. If music is desired, play familiar and calming instrumental music.

- Make sure the temperature is comfortable and the lighting is adequate.

- Make sure the dining chair is comfortable.

- Try using tablecloths or place mats that provide color contrast to place settings, such as a white plate on a dark blue place mat.

- Limit the number of items on the table to minimize distractions. Salt and pepper shakers, extra utensils, condiment jars, and flowers can take the person's attention away from eating. As with all challenging behaviors, it is important to observe what your relative needs to be successful. One person may play with a tablecloth, another person will not. One person may be able to use a napkin and another person may be so distracted by the color and texture of the napkin that she may forget to eat.

- As dementia progresses, it may become necessary to simplify the table setting with one eating utensil and one bowl or plate.

Other Considerations for Eating Challenges

- Keep in mind your relative's past eating habits. Did she always have a small appetite or eat large meals? Did she routinely eat snacks during certain times of the day? Did she often crave sweets?

- Being involved in meal preparation, seeing and smelling the food, setting the table may stimulate your relative's appetite.

- Giving your relative a choice about what she would like to eat may increase her interest in eating: *"Mom, what would you like for breakfast, oatmeal or scrambled eggs?"*

- Allow adequate time for your relative to eat and finish a meal. There are many steps in eating a meal: finding the food on the plate, recognizing the food, making decisions about how to eat and what to eat first, etc. A person with dementia often needs more time to process and complete each step and to finish her meal.

- Try showing your relative what you want her to do. In the later stages of dementia, people often forget how to eat, but they may be able to copy what another person is doing. Sit and eat with your relative, making sure you are in her field of vision. Show her what you want her to do: open your mouth, chew, swallow, etc.

- Make sure your relative is sitting a comfortable distance from the table and her food is within reach.

- Transfer your relative out of a wheelchair and into a dining chair when possible. Sitting in a wheelchair for long periods of time can be uncomfortable and even painful. This can affect a person's ability to focus and enjoy the food. If she must have a wheelchair, make it as comfortable as possible for her with pillows, and footrests, and by positioning the chair as close to the table as possible.

- Many challenges with eating are temporary and will change over time.

Adapting the dining environment can reduce stress and frustration.

MOUTH CARE: CARING FOR TEETH, GUMS AND DENTURES

MOUTH CARE:
CARING FOR TEETH, GUMS AND DENTURES

All of us need dental care every day. It is essential not only to the health of our teeth and gums, but vital to our overall health. With healthy teeth and gums, eating is more enjoyable and tooth decay and loss are often avoided. Oral hygiene is the practice of keeping one's mouth and gums healthy with regular, daily care. Without regular oral hygiene, we are at risk of infections, chewing problems, weight loss and increased vulnerability to other health conditions.

Most people continue to take care of teeth and brush regularly in the early stages of dementia. As dementia progresses, however, many people may not remember to brush their teeth or recognize the importance of good oral hygiene. It can often be challenging for care partners to know if their relative is keeping up with oral hygiene or is experiencing discomfort or pain. Here are some signs to watch for that may indicate that an evaluation by a dentist is needed:

- Wincing while chewing food or drinking a hot or cold beverage.

- Touching or pulling on mouth or cheek.

- Loss of appetite.

- Avoiding eating with other people.

- Refusing to have dentures in her mouth (due to sore or inflammation of gums).

- Refusing to open mouth when approached with a toothbrush.

- Swollen, reddened or bleeding gums.

- Bad breath that does not go away with regular brushing or with mouthwash.

A person with dementia may not remember to brush her teeth or recognize the importance of good oral hygiene.

As a care partner, you may find yourself needing to take a more active role in your relative's oral hygiene as her dementia progresses.

It can help to develop a dental care plan for your relative shortly after the diagnosis of dementia. Make a dental appointment for a thorough check-up to identify any problems that need attention. Ask your dentist about how often your relative will need dental visits.

As your relative's dementia progresses, dental care may be more challenging. Your relative may not accept having someone put a toothbrush in her mouth or remove her dentures. Trying to understand the causes of her resistance will be important in figuring out how to keep her mouth healthy.

Possible Physical, Medical and Emotional Causes of Poor Oral Hygiene

- Physical changes in the brain can result in poor oral hygiene.

  - Your relative may not remember to brush her teeth or the last time she brushed her teeth.

- A shortened attention span may prevent someone with dementia from completing the task of cleaning teeth or dentures.

- She may no longer have the ability to initiate oral care.

- She may no longer understand the sequence of steps needed to complete the task.

- Your relative may no longer recognize items that are needed for oral care: toothbrush, toothpaste, denture cleaner and cup, etc. (agnosia)

- She may not recognize or feel mouth or gum pain.

• Arthritis may make it difficult to hold a toothbrush, handle dental floss or clean dentures.

• Pain in knees and feet can make it difficult to walk to the sink or stand while performing oral care.

• Inflammation or infection of gums may be causing so much discomfort that she avoids brushing her teeth.

• Pain caused by broken or missing teeth may inhibit brushing.

• Ill-fitting dentures – often because they are old or the person has lost weight – may be irritating gums and preventing her from wanting to insert or remove them.

• Side effects of some medications, such as anti-depressants, can cause dry mouth, making it uncomfortable and sometimes painful to chew and swallow food.

• She may be embarrassed that she is no longer able to perform her own dental hygiene.

• Depression may cause your relative to lose interest in taking care of herself, including brushing her teeth.

• She may have a fear of choking.

• The individual may not have been taking care of her own oral hygiene prior to the onset of memory loss. Inadequate or no routine dental care often has not been performed due to the person's fear of dentists, or the inability to pay.

Strategies to Try for Possible Physical, Medical and Emotional Causes of Poor Oral Hygiene

• The first step in ensuring good dental care is to make an appointment with a dentist for a thorough check up of gums, broken or missing teeth, infection, etc. (See **Other Considerations** at the end of this section)

• Schedule an appointment with your relative's doctor if you suspect that pain or depression may be a problem. Successful treatment of these conditions can make a big difference in all activities of daily living.

• Schedule your relative's mouth and tooth care the same time every day. Think about her past routine: when and how often did she brush her teeth? Brushing teeth after meals and before bedtime may be a familiar time for many people. On the other hand, if she is too tired to cooperate at bedtime, find a time of day when she is more rested.

• Divide the task of cleaning teeth into several steps if your relative is unable to complete the task at one time. After breakfast, ask your relative to swish water in her mouth to remove food particles. After lunch, try brushing teeth. Oral hygiene at bedtime is also important, if possible.

- Use a soft bristle toothbrush. Your relative may be more accepting and comfortable with softer bristles.

- Try a large handled toothbrush if your relative has hand, finger or wrist pain. These can be purchased at many pharmacies or online. Or you can adapt a regular size toothbrush handle by inserting a foam hair roller on it. Some children's toothbrushes have larger handles and are easier for people to grip.

- Try a smaller toothbrush if your relative is hesitant to open her mouth. A child's toothbrush is often a good option.

- Try an electric toothbrush if thorough cleaning is a challenge. Some people may accept it and others may reject it because it is unfamiliar or frightening.

- Try interdental or "go between brushes" if she is uncomfortable flossing. Several types are available at local pharmacies and online.

- Wrap a moistened gauze pad around your finger and sweep through her mouth at the end of oral care. This practice can capture food particles that cause bacteria if left in the mouth, and is good both for people with teeth and those with dentures.

- For someone who wears dentures:
  - Remove dentures for at least four hours a day to let the gums breathe. The best time to do this for many people is at bedtime because the person will feel embarrassed to be seen without her dentures.
  - Check for sores, reddened or swollen areas on her gums.

- For dry mouth:
  - Try sugar free gum or hard candy to alleviate dry mouth, if there is no fear of choking.
  - Offer your relative sips of water throughout the day.
  - Ask your dentist about products for dry mouth. You can also google "over the counter dry mouth products" and you will find a variety available.
  - Provide the dentist with a complete list of medications and ask if there are medications that could be causing dry mouth. If the dentist is unfamiliar with all medications, consult your relative's doctor.

- Try assisting your relative while she is sitting upright in the chair if there is a swallowing problem or a fear of choking.

- Try toothpastes without fluoride. Fluoride toothpastes foam and can cause coughing and choking. Ask your dentists for recommendations of non-fluoride cleaners.

Possible Environmental Causes of Poor Oral Hygiene

- There is not enough light in the bathroom to locate toothbrush, toothpaste, denture cleaner and glass, etc.

- Your relative is distracted by clutter in the bathroom.

- The bathroom is too cold.

- There is not enough contrast between the counter and the items needed for oral hygiene so that she has difficulty locating them.

- The person can not remember how to turn the water on or off.

- She is not comfortable in the bathroom or cannot stand at the sink comfortably.

- The bathroom is unfamiliar and she is afraid to be alone there.

Strategies to Try for Possible Environmental Causes of Poor Oral Hygiene

- Provide brighter lighting or additional lighting if the area is dim.

- Warm up the bathroom ahead of time.

- Try to schedule oral care during daylight hours.

- De-clutter the bathroom. This can minimize distractions and may help the person focus on her oral hygiene.

- Attach labels to toothpaste, toothbrush, denture cleaner and denture cup, if she is able to read.

- Place dental care items on a towel of contrasting color. This may help your relative locate what she needs to perform her dental care.

- Stay with your relative in the bathroom while oral care is being done if she is fearful of being alone. Or stay outside the bathroom door and let her know you are available to help if she needs it. *"Mom, I am right here. Let me know if you need any help."*

- Perform dental care where your relative is most comfortable if she is not able to walk to the bathroom. This could be at the kitchen sink, the dining table after a meal or at a table in her bedroom. Bring the toothbrush, toothpaste, drinking glass and basin in which to spit to her, making sure all supplies are within her reach.

> As Teresa's dementia progressed, her partner Monica noticed she was not brushing her teeth regularly. When Monica would remind her, Teresa would nod and say, "I will in a minute," but she would not remember and her teeth were not getting brushed. Monica tried to have Teresa brush right after she used the toilet, thinking it would be easier for her to do both tasks in one trip to the bathroom, but Teresa could not stand at the sink as long as it took to brush her teeth. Monica thought about where Teresa would be most comfortable and decided to try having her brush her teeth at the table after her meal. She brought everything that was needed on a tray and said, "Before you get up and move to your chair, I thought you might like to brush your teeth. Here is your toothbrush, toothpaste, water and a basin." Although it took several attempts, Monica was relieved when Teresa did eventually brush her teeth after every meal.

- Play calming and familiar instrumental music before your relative enters the bathroom and throughout oral care. Don't play music she might try to sing along to, however, as this will interfere.

Other Considerations for Good Mouth Care

- Schedule professional cleaning appointments as often as you can for as long as you can. A dentist is able to examine and clean teeth and gums in a way that you or your relative might not be able to do.

- Find the right dentist. Although there are many dentists who care for older adults, many dentists are not trained or experienced in providing dental care to people with dementia. If your relative does not have a dentist, call some of the assisted living homes and nursing homes in your area and ask for the names of the dentists who see their residents with dementia. Your local dental society may also be able to furnish names of dentists who work with older adults. Also dentists who work with special needs children often are good with people with dementia as well.

- Prior to the dental appointment:

  - Notify the dentist ahead of time about your relative's diagnosis to make sure the dentist is comfortable and qualified to care for your relative.

  - Tell the dentist if your relative is able to maintain her own dental care or if she needs reminders or assistance.

  - Report any concerns that you or your relative might have.

  - Tell the dentist about any symptoms related to her dementia that might occur during the dental appointment: the inability to report symptoms or locate pain, restlessness, ability to follow instructions or answer questions, etc.

  - Ask the dentist about the expected length of the appointment. If you are concerned that your relative might be unable to sit in the dental chair for the required length of time, ask if the needed procedure can be completed in two appointments. Some dentists may suggest a mild sedative for patients with dementia when a lengthy or invasive dental procedure is necessary. Consult your relative's primary care doctor about the dentist's recommendation(s).

  - Schedule the dental appointment at your relative's best time of day.

> *Grace began to notice that her husband Otto was not brushing his teeth regularly until one day he began rubbing his jaw and wouldn't eat. Grace looked in his mouth and saw that his gums were swollen and red. She was worried about getting him to the dentist and how he would do once he was there. She called the dentist, explained the situation and told the dentist that Otto had Alzheimer's disease. She cautioned that Otto might not be cooperative. Otto did quite well during the abbreviated appointment. Grace felt that the dentist was more comfortable because of the background information she gave him.*

- On the day of the appointment:

  - Avoid possible wait time by calling ahead and asking if the dentist is on time.

  - Consider how long in advance to tell your relative about the dental appointment if you think this will cause her to be anxious.

  - Ask the dentist if you can stay in the examination room if you think your presence will help calm your relative during the dental procedure.

Communication Tips and Strategies for Good Mouth Care

- Invite your relative to brush her teeth with you. *"Mom, I am going to brush my teeth before I go to bed. Do you want to join me?"* This is often is more comfortable than saying *"It is time to brush your teeth, mom."*

- Involve her in performing her own oral hygiene as much as possible. There are often some steps in oral care that a person can do for herself, if given the chance.

- Give simple step-by-step instructions. *"Wilma, here is your toothbrush. Hold it while I put toothpaste on it. I will turn on the water for you so you can wet your toothbrush."*

- Give your relative enough time. There are multiple steps in oral care that can take the person with dementia more time to complete than we expect. She may need time to process what to do with the toothpaste, how to pick up the tooth brush and to turn on the water, etc.

- Cue and praise your relative for the job she is doing, even if she is not doing it perfectly. *"Frances, you are doing a great job of cleaning your front teeth. Can you brush your back teeth also or would you like me to help you?"* Recognize that you may have to go back and clean areas that are missed, if possible.

- Try the "hand over hand" technique to guide the toothbrush to her mouth to get her started and to help her with all steps of dental care, if necessary.

- Try again later if your relative resists your assistance or suggestion.

References

Dolan, T. A., Atchison, K., & Huynh, T. N. (2005). Access to dental care among older adults in the United States. Journal of Dental Education, 69(9), 961-974.

Lamster, I. & Ahluwalia, K.P. (2014). Oral health care affects quality of life. Today's Geriatric Medicine, 7(6), 22.

Mouth Care Without a Battle, video, Cecil G. Sheps Center, University of North Carolina. http://www.mouthcarewithoutabattle.org.

WHEN YOU GOTTA GO: HELPING YOUR RELATIVE IN THE BATHROOM

WHEN YOU GOTTA GO:
HELPING YOUR RELATIVE IN THE BATHROOM

Difficulty with toileting is one of the more stressful situations that people with dementia and their caregivers may face. For the person this can be humiliating and for families it can be both heartbreaking and terribly frustrating. Families may find this problem very embarrassing, especially in public places.

How we think and talk about these issues can impact how we handle them. If we shame or scold the person, she is more likely to become angry or agitated. Matter-of-fact, unemotional approaches tend to work best. Research on aggressive behaviors and dementia has shown that aggression tends to surface during personal care – for example when someone is being helped in the bathroom – when people feel most vulnerable and humiliated.

Helping someone be as independent as possible with toileting can be time consuming. A person's self-esteem is negatively affected by increased dependence and positively affected by helping them remain as independent as possible.

Medical personnel use the term incontinence, urinary or fecal, which essentially means difficulty controlling one's urine and bowels resulting in soiling oneself. Not every person with dementia becomes incontinent, but it is not uncommon. Urinary incontinence in particular is quite common; in later stages of dementia bowel incontinence may become a problem.

Possible Physical, Medical and Emotional Causes of Incontinence

- Brain changes from dementia can cause:

  - Memory loss. People sometimes forget how to find the bathroom. Or they may be distracted on the way to the bathroom and forget what they were going to do.

  - Not recognizing objects. This can make it hard to recognize the toilet.

  - Loss of communication between the brain and bladder or bowels. The urge or signal to go to the bathroom may no longer be understood or received correctly by the brain.

  - Apathy (lack of interest). This often occurs in severe depression and some forms of dementia and can result in people not responding to the need to go to the bathroom.

- Stress incontinence (sneezing, coughing, laughing) is a common cause of urinary leaking in older women.

- Urge incontinence (recognizing the need to urinate but unable to hold it until she gets to the bathroom) is also common in older women.

- Infections in older women are also a common cause of urinary incontinence. These include urinary tract infections, urethritis (inflammation of the urethra, the tube that carries urine from the bladder to outside the body) and vaginitis, (inflammation of the vagina that causes pain and itching).

- Enlarged prostate in men can cause retention of urine. Men are especially susceptible to infections after prostate surgery.

- Constipation or fecal impaction can contribute to both urinary and fecal incontinence. "Constipation is when you are not passing stool as often as you normally do. Your stool becomes hard and dry, and it is difficult to pass. Fecal impaction is often seen in people who have had constipation for a long time and have been using laxatives. Impaction is even more likely when the laxatives are stopped suddenly. The muscles of the intestines forget how to move stool or feces on their own." (www.nim.nih.gov/medlineplus/ency/article/000230.htm)

- Chronic illnesses can make it difficult to get to the bathroom. These include diabetes, Parkinson's disease, arthritis, strokes or any condition that limits mobility and/or causes chronic pain. With Parkinson's disease, slowness and rigidity can contribute to problems. Also, constipation is a noted and common problem for people with Parkinson's disease. People who have had strokes may have "one-sided neglect" where they are unaware of one side of the body. This can cause mobility and spatial problems.

- Knee pain can make it difficult for the person to get up from a seated position and cause the person to avoid wanting to go to the bathroom.

- Neuropathy (numbness, weakness, pain) in feet or other foot conditions may make it painful to walk to the bathroom.

- Being exhausted can make it hard to get to the bathroom quickly. Or sometimes the person may be sleeping soundly and wet herself.

- Dehydration – insufficient intake of fluids – can cause irritation of the bladder. Dehydration also can cause incontinence by lowering or eliminating the signal to urinate.

- Some liquids increase the need to urinate. Fluids having a diuretic effect, such as coffee, tea, cocoa, beer and colas, can affect control of urine. A diuretic is a substance that increases the production of urine. There are medications that are diuretics, but common fluids listed above also can have this effect.

- Medications can affect bladder and bowel control, including medications used to control behavior. If incontinence becomes a problem, discuss medications with your relative's physician and/or pharmacist.

- Observe the toileting pattern of your relative during the day and at night. Try and toilet just before her expected time.

- Fear can contribute to problems with toileting in several ways: She may be fearful or anxious about having to partially undress in front of another person. She may be fearful about leaving a comfortable chair or bed, getting lost, or being out of the sight of her caregiver. She may be afraid of falling. Improper footwear, stairs, throw rugs, and low toilets can all lead to falls.

- Anxiety can also be a contributor. Some people are so anxious about incontinence or about the presence of another person that it interferes with going to the bathroom appropriately.

- The person feels rushed. Sometimes when we are feeling rushed, we rush our relatives in the bathroom. Most people have difficulty going to the bathroom on command.

Strategies to Try for Possible Physical, Medical, and Emotional Causes of Incontinence

- Try keeping a log for a few days. Follow the guidelines in the **Becoming a Detective** section. See if you can find a pattern to the behavior. A few questions for you to think about that pertain specifically to incontinence are:

  - Do accidents happen only at certain times of day or night?

  - Did the incontinence begin suddenly?

  - Can you identify warning signs that your relative needs to go to the bathroom? For example, some people fiddle with their pants or belt when they need to urinate. Some grab their crotches. Others begin pacing.

- Have a thorough medical examination to discover any possible infections or medication problems that may be contributing to the incontinence.

- Consider a continence diagnostic evaluation if the cause of the incontinence is still unknown. This would involve a series of tests that can determine how well the urinary system is functioning. However, these procedures are uncomfortable and expensive and the benefits need to be carefully evaluated on an individual basis.

- If possible, avoid medications that have side effects of constipation or excessive urination.

- Avoid overuse of laxatives and enemas.

- Report a fever that lasts more than 24 hours to the doctor. Urinary tract infections (UTI) are often accompanied by fevers and can be dangerous if left untreated. On the other hand, be aware that UTIs can cause behavior change as the main symptom without fever or other obvious signs. Strong smelling and dark colored urine can be signs of infection.

- Be aware that there are medications to treat incontinence but they do have side effects and should be carefully monitored. Side effects can include dry mouth, vision problems and increased confusion.

- Monitor the use of diuretics. If a diuretic is being taken, it is important to carefully consider the times of day when it is given to minimize incontinence.

- Be sure the person is drinking adequate fluids - a minimum of 6 to 8 glasses daily. Many people with dementia forget to drink or may no longer recognize the sensation of thirst; paradoxically, not drinking enough fluid can lead to urinary problems. A wide variety of substances act as fluids, including fruits, JELL-O®, Popsicles® or ice cream. Also, try herbal teas and decaffeinated coffee since caffeine, colas, and grapefruit juice can act as diuretics.

- Set up a regular schedule with specific times for the person to have something to drink, e.g., with meals and three daily snacks.

- Take the person to the toilet before and after meals and immediately before going to bed.

- Monitor liquid intake in the evening. Some families have found that limiting liquids after supper helps with nighttime incontinence. However, some medical experts discourage this practice, believing that many peoples' bladders do not function properly because of inadequate fluid intake.

- Make sure the person actually urinates before getting off the toilet.

- Try a commode on the ground floor so that she does not have to climb the stairs if that is difficult.

- If a person is having trouble urinating, try giving a glass of water to drink while sitting on the toilet, letting the water run in the sink, or giving the person a glass of water with a straw to blow bubbles. Sometimes flushing the toilet helps. It may be helpful to gently rub the person's lower back to stimulate reflexes or to stroke the lower abdomen over the bladder.

- Reassure your relative that you know this is difficult or embarrassing.

Possible Environmental Causes of Incontinence

- The distance to the bathroom may be too far.

- The bed is too high or too low making it difficult for the person to get up.

- The floor surface of the bathroom is disorienting. A person with dementia may perceive a dark floor surface or dark tiles as holes and be fearful of entering the bathroom. A person with impaired depth perception may be fearful of negotiating the changing floor surfaces from room to room.

- The toilet and the surrounding areas – floor and walls - are the same color, making it difficult to distinguish the toilet. As a person's depth perception and visual recognition change, sometimes it becomes difficult to see the toilet.

- The person is confused about the proper receptacle. Sometimes people try to use the sink or a wastebasket because they are having trouble recognizing the toilet.

- The toilet is too low for ease or comfort.

- Doors to the bathroom or other rooms are too difficult to open.

- Poor lighting can cause difficulty in finding the bathroom or locating the toilet inside the bathroom.

- Mirrors are sometimes frightening or disorienting in the later stages of dementia. A person may no longer recognize herself and may think someone is watching her.

- There are no orientation cues or signs to help find the way or identify bathroom.

- Lack of privacy in adult day programs or residential care, in particular, may lead to incontinence because the person feels so embarrassed.

Strategies for Possible Environmental Causes of Incontinence

- If the bathroom is too far away, consider using a portable commode or a wheelchair. Leave the top off the commode so she can easily identify it as a toilet. Make sure the commode is stable.

- Alter the height of the bed if that seems to be a problem.

- Ask your physician's office if a prescription can be written if you need equipment. Medicare pays for some medical equipment.

- Use a raised toilet seat with handrails to make it easier for a person to get on and off the toilet.

- If the floor surface is causing fear or disorientation, reassure your relative, demonstrate that it is safe to step on, and help her over the threshold.

- If the person is having trouble with finding the toilet seat, try a colored one. A dark toilet seat provides contrast to the white toilet bowl, making it easier for some people with depth perception problems.

- Cover the sink and waste basket if those are being used instead of the toilet.

- Try leaving doors open and improving the lighting as needed to make the path to the bathroom as clear as possible.

- Cover or remove mirrors if they are distracting or disturbing the person.

- Try using signs. Put a sign on the bathroom door using a familiar word such as "bathroom" printed in large letters. If the person is no longer able to read, try a photograph of a toilet.

- Give your relative a bell to ring when she is finished.

- Give as much privacy as possible, while still offering the help that is needed.

Strategies for Night Time Incontinence

- Try putting a portable commode next to the bed.

- Try urinals and bedpans if it is difficult for the person to get out of bed. For men, there are spill proof urinals that can be kept in bed.

- Make sure there are nightlights or other adequate light in the bathroom, hallway and bedroom.

- Make sure there is no clutter (throw rugs, chairs) lying in the pathway to the toilet. Falls often occur on the way to the bathroom at night.

- Make sure slippers are not too loose, floppy or slippery.

- Use disposable pads and rubberized flannel sheets to protect bedding.

- Try using a draw sheet in bed. This is a regular sheet folded in half lengthwise and tucked in across the bed. It can hold a plastic pad in place between it. Should the person have an accident, there is only the draw sheet and the pad to change.

Other Possible Causes of Incontinence

- The task of going to the bathroom alone has become too complicated. The person is not getting the help needed for undressing, sitting on the toilet, wiping or rising from the toilet.

- She may have lost the ability to communicate her needs. The person may no longer have the language skills to express the need or to understand the caregiver's question.

- The instructions are too complicated. The caregiver may not be giving simple or clear enough instructions.

- Clothing may be too complicated for your relative to manage.

Communication Strategies for Incontinence

Hiroko Tanaka often refused to go to the bathroom when her husband, Jun, asked her to. Frequently she ended up wetting herself and the chair where she spent most of her time. Jun tried keeping a log for a few days and learned that his wife was usually incontinent around 10 am and 2 pm, several hours after meals. He tried various communication strategies and finally found one that worked most of the time. He would reach out his hand to her and say, "Come." Usually she would stand up and they walked together down the hall, talking about the pictures on the wall. When they got to the bathroom, he would lead her to the toilet and say, "Now I'm going to help you with your clothes." He would pull down her pants and say, "Please sit, Hiroko." Then he would wait outside the door for her. The simplicity of his instructions seemed to work well for her. Jun concluded that she had not understood much of what he said in the past, leading her to refuse.

- Consider ways of inviting the person to the bathroom in a friendly, matter-of-fact manner. For example, *"Come, walk down the hall with me and keep me company."* Or, *"I'm on my way to the bathroom. Please join me."*

- Don't invite a refusal. *"Would you like to go to the bathroom?"* is likely to be met with a *"No!"* When a person is asked if she has to go to the toilet, she may feel embarrassed or insulted and say no.

- When language comprehension is difficult, simplify the steps involved.

- Be sure you give the person simple but adequate warning and explanation about what is happening. *"Mary, I am going to pull your pants down so I can help you."* You want to warn, reassure, and explain what you are doing.

- Use the terms or words that are familiar and that the person uses. Some people may use words from childhood or slang like "pee," "tinkle," or "take a leak."

- Reassure the person if she has an accident. Even severely impaired people do care when they are incontinent. Saying something like, *"Soon, everything will be all right,"* or *"Don't worry, everything will be fine,"* may help.

- Avoid reprimanding the person if there has been an accident.

Clothing Strategies and Incontinence Products

- Simplify clothing. Try Velcro® tape instead of zippers or buttons. Try elastic waistbands for pants or wrap around skirts.

- Use underpants when possible. They can serve as a reminder to stay dry and as a stimulus to use the toilet when wet. Padded underwear is often acceptable to people where disposable garments that look like diapers may not be.

- Remove underwear in the drawer and replace with disposable or padded garments.

- Change clothes immediately when they are wet. Try not to let the person become accustomed to wet clothes.

- Select clothing that is washable and does not need ironing.

- Buy washable or easily cleaned shoes for someone who is incontinent.

- Keep disposable gloves handy.

- Always keep spare clothing and supplies in your car. Incontinence away from home can be particularly upsetting, so be prepared!

- There are many incontinence products available now through medical supply stores, pharmacies, and online. Some are disposable; others are washable and reusable. These range from pull up disposable pants to washable cotton underwear with built in pads of various strengths; these are usually sold by waist and hip size. It is worth trying several products to find one that works well for your situation.

Bowel Incontinence or Problems with Constipation

- Check with the doctor if this is a new problem, since both diarrhea and constipation can be symptoms of illness. Also there are a number of medications, such as some used for pain, that can cause constipation.

- Try and establish a routine to help keep track of the person's bowel movements. Because of memory impairment, people with dementia often forget when they last had a bowel movement. The urge to go is often the strongest the first hour after breakfast.

- Pay attention to body language. People with constipation cannot always verbalize the problem but may rub or hold their stomach. Some people may be uncomfortable sitting down when constipated or impacted.

- Try a high-fiber diet adding bran to cereal or muffins; be sure there is plenty of liquid along with the fiber or constipation may worsen.

- Be sure your relative is getting plenty of fruits and vegetables in her diet.

- Be sure she is drinking at least 6 to 8 glasses of fluid daily.

- Make sure the person gets plenty of regular exercise.

- Ask your physician about stool softeners. These are sometimes necessary when people have had a history of constipation or are taking medications that can be constipating.

- Ask for a referral to a dietician if problems persist.

- Sometimes people in later stages of dementia will get feces on their hands or get it on the walls or sink. This is usually a result of trying to clean themselves or misunderstanding what is happening. Again it can be helpful to try to understand the cause of this behavior. Although you may feel extremely upset, it is helpful to stay calm and matter of fact and not scold the person.

Other Considerations Related to Bowel Incontinence or Constipation

- Skin care is extremely important. Skin that is often wet or exposed to feces can begin to break down and cause sores. Wash the skin after any accident. There are special products available which act as both soaps and skin conditioners. Also there are over the counter products to use if the skin begins to break down. Talk with your doctor about what options might be best for your relative.

- Set up a regular toileting schedule, every two or three hours based on what you observe about your relative's schedule.

- Respect the privacy and dignity of the person who may be having problems with incontinence as much as possible. None of us would choose to be in that position.

- Some people may hide soiled clothing, wrap up feces or soiled bedding. Often these behaviors are caused by embarrassment at the incontinence or a desire to clean it up without knowing any longer how to do so. She may not remember hiding clothing and will genuinely believe that she did not do it.

- Family members and other caregivers also may feel embarrassed or awkward when assisting with toileting and should be aware that these are normal feelings. Sometimes people find cleaning up to be a very difficult and unpleasant task and may gag. Try to be calm and reassuring and recognize that both of you probably feel quite uncomfortable in this situation. An air freshener may help with the smell.

- Look for family friendly restrooms in public places. When either the caregiver or the person with dementia must go in the wrong sex bathroom:

  - Ask someone to stand at the door while you assist the person.

  - Consider posting a sign on the restroom door.

  - Have a card handy that says, *"Thank you for understanding. My relative has dementia and needs assistance."*

- If your relative is particularly hyperactive or anxious, allow her to get up and down from the toilet a few times. Music can sometimes have a calming effect. Try distracting her with a magazine or something to hold, such as a knotted pair of socks, to keep her busy while sitting on the toilet.

- Purchase washable chair cushion covers. Or, put garbage bags over cushions to waterproof them.

- In the later stages of dementia, the use of indwelling catheters is rarely recommended. Infections frequently develop and lead to other problems. Catheters are necessary only when the person has significant skin sores or when there are other overriding medical reasons.

- In choosing adult day programs or residential care, notice how incontinence is managed. Ask questions about how they handle incontinence and whether they have regular toileting schedules. Pay attention to odor and appearance of the residence, keeping in mind that any place may occasionally have an odor if they have a number of incontinent residents. For a nursing home, ask about their track record with bedsores. You can also look this up on the medicare.gov website under inspection reports for individual nursing homes.

OVER AND OVER AGAIN: REPETITIVE BEHAVIORS

OVER AND OVER AGAIN: REPETITIVE BEHAVIORS

Repetitive behaviors can be among the most stressful and irritating behaviors for family caregivers. A relative with memory loss may forget that she asked the same question several times, making it challenging for caregivers to respond in a calm and reassuring voice.

In later stages of dementia, tapping fingers, rubbing arms or thighs, fidgeting with things, pacing or rocking back and forth are common repetitive behaviors. You may not recognize that these are often a means of self comfort. These repetitive behaviors are known as perseveration: "A persistent repetition of a word, gesture or act that is associated with brain disease." (Random House ©, 2015)

Possible Physical, Medical, and Emotional Causes of Repetitive Behaviors

- Physical changes in the brain can cause:

  - The person with dementia to no longer remember that she is repeating herself.

  - The inability to stop a repetitive action.

  - Anxiety or tension often caused by the disorientation and memory loss that come with dementia.

  - A person to no longer recognize when to stop doing something. She may continue spooning her soup bowl when there is no more soup in the bowl.

- Pain can cause people with dementia to rock, pace or move in other rhythmic ways when they are uncomfortable.

- When a person feels depressed, repetitive actions or gestures may be the only way she can express herself or cope with certain places, situations or people.

- Feeling bored or unsure of what to do can prompt some people with dementia to repeatedly ask, *"What do I do now?"*

- She may be trying to express a need. A person who is hungry may constantly ask, *"What's for lunch?"* Or *"Is it time to eat?"* Someone who needs to go to the bathroom may fidget with his belt buckle or her pants. A person who feels cold may repeatedly check closets for a blanket or a sweater.

- A person with dementia may be trying to express an emotion, such as fear, anger or insecurity. Wringing her hands or tapping fingers on a table may be a way that she is trying to comfort herself.

- Your relative may be feeling vulnerable or anxious and need reassurance, especially in a new or unfamiliar environment or with unfamiliar people.

- She may be trying to be social and keep a conversation going by saying the same things repeatedly.

- A person with memory loss may be doing something that relates to a former job. A former security guard may constantly check doors to make sure they are locked or pace the halls to make sure everyone is safe.

- Your relative may be pacing because she needs to use the toilet or needs to exercise.

- Your relative may misunderstand what is happening, or what another person is doing. This may be expressed in questions such as, *"What are you doing?"*

- There is some evidence that individuals with Frontotemporal dementia (FTD) are more likely to exhibit repetitive movements than people with other forms of dementia (Mendez, et al., 2005). Obsessive behaviors, rubbing or tapping parts of the body, repetitive facial movements all appear to be more common in FTD or when there is significant damage to the frontal lobe part of the brain related to Alzheimer's disease or other forms of dementia.

- Side effects of some psychotropic medications (used for treating psychiatric symptoms, see **Glossary**) can cause repetitive movements such as repeatedly sticking the tongue in and out or chewing motions. This is called tardive dyskinesia and is an unfortunate side effect of some medications. At times it improves when the medication is discontinued, but it can be permanent.

Strategies to Try for Possible Physical, Medical and Emotional Causes of Repetitive Behaviors

Repetitive movements may be more upsetting to you than to your relative, who may be unaware of them.

- Redirect the person to a favorite activity or a favorite food.

- Try scheduling physical activities during the day. Take your relative for a walk, toss a ball, do chair exercises if a milder form of exercise is needed. Movement can reduce stress, tension, frustration and may help improve her mood.

- For repetitive mouth movements, rubbing hands together or on legs, tapping, and repeated actions of various kinds:

  - Schedule a medical examination to review all medications and assess for illness, pain or depression.

  - Occupy the person's hands. Give the person something to hold: a soft blanket, a doll, a stuffed animal or a nerf ball.

  - Try distraction with music, food, exercise, etc.

  - Offer an activity that requires repetition such as folding laundry, dusting, sweeping, raking, etc.

  - Offer chewing gum if there is not a danger of choking.

- When a person is stuck on one step of a task, repeating it again and again (perseveration):

  - Try showing the person what you are requesting. Some people may understand and respond better when they are shown than when given verbal instructions.

  - Be sure to allow enough time, so the person doesn't feel rushed through the task.

- Use touch and pointing to gently move on to the next step, e.g., touch arm that goes in the sleeve, point to the sleeve.

- Keep instructions simple and short. Using consistent instructions throughout the activity may help the person understand and participate in the activity.

- Try to understand that repetitive motions may be necessary before the person can move on to the next part of the task.

- Be aware that interrupting the repetitive movement may be very annoying to the person.

• While it is important to try the above strategies, it is also important to recognize that repetitive behaviors related to the changes in your relative's brain may not ever go away. At times these repetitive movements are more upsetting to you than to your relative, who may be unaware of them.

Possible Environmental Causes of Repetitive Actions, Statements and Questions

• Environmental cues can give the wrong message. Coats, shoes, purses, umbrellas, etc., can prompt the person with dementia to repeatedly ask, *"Is it time to go now?"*

• Being separated from a loved one can cause constant questions such as, *"Where's Tom?"*

• Too much stimulus in the environment, such as too many people or too much activity or noise can cause a person to say, *"Let's go now. Let's go now."*

Environmental Strategies to Try When Your Relative Asks Questions Repeatedly

• Remove things in the environment that may trigger repetitive questions, such as the items listed above.

• Try to reduce the amount of stimulus in the environment or take the person away from the people, noise and activities to see if these factors are possible triggers.

• Remind your relative with brief, simple statements. *"Your daughter will be home from work soon."* Don't overload her with long explanations or try to reason with her.

• Give the person a note to hold. *"I am at my Rotary meeting. I will be home at 5:30. Your husband, Ralph."*

• Use memory aids. Signs, large numeral clocks, calendars, and schedules can help orient some people and reduce repetitive questions such as *"What time is it?"* or *"What time is Sally coming?"*

• Use simple written reminders with people who can still read. Large signs might say, *"Dinner is at 5:30 p.m."* or *"Your son Mark will be visiting at 3:30 today."* Posting notes next to a clock may help those who can read both the note and the clock.

- Try posting a white board in the kitchen or living room with the daily schedule written on it. This may help a person with dementia know what to expect. Some people will remember to look at the white board; others may need to be reminded to look at what is planned for the day.

Strategies to Try for Other Causes of Repetitive Behaviors

- Use a calm voice when responding to her repeated questions. Frustration or anger in your voice is likely to escalate your relative's anxiety. If you find it difficult to conceal your frustration, try remaining silent. By remaining silent, anger and frustration cannot be conveyed in your voice.

- Try ignoring the behavior or question. If there is no response or reinforcement, the behavior may stop. However, some people may be very upset when they are ignored and become more agitated. For others, ignoring eventually works. Be patient while you learn what works and what doesn't work.

- Try a gentle touch when a verbal response does not help. Sometimes a hug, holding hands or a gentle shoulder massage may be more reassuring than words.

- Try soothing music that is familiar to the person. There is research that indicates music can be helpful in reducing agitation and may stop repetitive actions, at least for a while (Sung & Chang, 2005).

- Respond to the emotion instead of the specific statement or question. The person may simply need reassurance or attention. *"Betty, I am going to stay here with you all day. You can let me know if you need anything."*

- Do not discuss plans with the person – appointments, visitors or outings - until just prior to an event if this causes anxiety. Knowing of an event too far ahead of time can cause agitation and repeated questions. If the person remembers an appointment has been scheduled but does not remember the time of the appointment, she may become anxious and repeatedly ask, *"When do I go to the doctor?"* There is no hard and fast rule here – some people respond well to information ahead of time, while others ask questions over and over.

> *Charlie told his wife Abigail that she had a doctor's appointment "tomorrow at 1 PM." Abigail was so anxious about the appointment that she got out of bed the next day at 5 AM and paced around the house, repeatedly asking, "When are we leaving?" On the way to the doctor's office, Abigail's anxiety increased to the point that Charlie had to pull over to the side of the road so he could calm her down. He decided to skip the appointment and go home. Abigail calmed down once she was home. The next time Abigail had a doctor's appointment, Charlie told Abigail she was going to see her doctor when they were only a few minutes away from the doctor's office.*

- Do not remind the person with memory loss that she has asked the same question before as this may upset her. Although it is difficult not to grow impatient, it is rarely helpful to point out the repetitions. It is the rare person who accepts reminders gracefully; more often individuals become defensive or angry. It is better to repeat the answer patiently or try one of the adaptations (white board, note, etc.) suggested above.

- Pacing may indicate that your relative needs to exercise, especially if she has been physically active throughout her life. Finding a safe place to walk regularly and building exercise into the daily routine may be helpful.

- Pacing back and forth may mean your relative has to go to the bathroom but is not able to tell you or is unable to find the toilet. Ask her if she needs a toilet. Gently direct her to the bathroom. A picture outside of the bathroom door may help orient the person and reduce her anxiety. (See **When You Gotta Go** for suggestions about this.)

- If an activity is often repeated, explore whether it may be related to an emotional memory from the past when the person felt scared or anxious.

> *Jackie's mother, Helen, sang the song Stella Stellini for a couple of hours almost every afternoon. Jackie tried to involve her in other activities, but all Helen wanted to do was sing this one song. Jackie was becoming very frustrated and annoyed until Jackie's sister told her that this lullaby had special meaning to their mother. When Helen was five years old she was temporarily separated from her mother when they landed in America and she sang Stella Stellini to comfort herself. Knowing this, Jackie began singing with Helen and reassured her that she would stay with Helen. With Jackie by her side, Helen felt safe and would sometimes sing softer, hum or stop singing.*

Other Considerations for Repetitive Actions and Questions

- Keep a log or diary to help determine possible causes of repetitive questions or actions. Does the behavior occur at a certain time of day or night? Are there particular people or events that often precede the behavior? Could the person be hungry? Cold or hot? In pain? Tired? In need of a bathroom?

- Take note of whether the behavior is occurring when your relative is separated from a loved one. When a loved one is not in sight, a person with dementia may feel frightened and agitated, causing the person to repeatedly ask, *"Where are you?"* Or *"What are you doing?"* Having the caregiver be within sight may help the person feel calm and more secure. Sometimes giving the person a photograph to hold or posting one in a familiar place can help.

- Give your full attention and respond to your relative's emotional needs. Sometimes people with dementia have lost the ability to know how to get attention and may be using questions as an attention getting device. If this is so, giving them attention and responding to their emotional needs can sometimes break the cycle of repetition for a while. A person may feel alone and anxious even when there is a familiar person nearby.

- Talking about or counting money repeatedly may be an expression of feeling loss of control. Try giving the person a small amount of money to keep in a wallet or a purse. Giving the person a note that explains her money is safe in the bank, with her financial advisor, etc., may also help.

- Joining your relative in an activity such as dancing, walking or other recreational activities may help the person feel less alone.

- Establishing a routine of activities that your relative enjoys and feels good about doing can help decrease anxiety that may be leading to repetitive behaviors.

- Try alternating active and quiet activities throughout the day. Schedule active exercises when the person is most rested or has the need to be active.

- Caregivers often have trouble believing that their relative is not purposely repeating questions in order to annoy them. This is rarely, if ever, the case. More likely, people with dementia are trying unsuccessfully to feel a sense of control over their lives.

- Remind yourself that people with dementia do not have the ability to remember because of changes in the brain. To you a question, story or comment is repetitive. To the person with dementia, it is the first time she has asked the question, expressed a concern or told you a story.

- Sometimes, despite our best efforts, repetitive questions or movements will not stop. If the repetitive behavior is not stressful or a safety threat to the person with dementia, it may help to recognize this as part of the disease. A change of attitude can sometimes help a caregiver cope with repetitive behaviors.

References

Mendez, M. F., Perryman, K. M., Miller, B. L., Swartz, J. R., & Cummings, J. L. (1997). Compulsive behaviors as presenting symptoms of frontotemporal dementia, Journal of Geriatric Psychiatry and Neurology, 10(4), 154-157.

Sung, H. C., & Chang, A. M. (2005). Use of preferred music to decrease agitated behaviours in older people with dementia: a review of the literature, Journal of Clinical Nursing, 14(9), 1133-1140.

THERE'S NO PLACE LIKE HOME: WHEN YOUR RELATIVE WANTS TO GO HOME

THERE'S NO PLACE LIKE HOME:
WHEN YOUR RELATIVE WANTS TO GO HOME

"Wanting to go home" seems to be one of the most frustrating and challenging behaviors for both family members and staff, and often requires a great deal of tact and creativity.

"I want to go home" is a phrase that people often voice in the middle and later stages of dementia. Families may struggle with this behavior while their loved one is living at home, attending a day program or following a move to a residential care setting. For this reason, we have included some considerations for families to try in these settings or to suggest to staff who work in these settings.

Where is Home? What is Home?

Wanting to go home is an expression that can have many different meanings besides wanting to return to a specific physical place. This requires us to go beyond the words to understand what the person is feeling and might need. Wanting to go home may be a phase that eventually passes as the illness progresses.

- "Home" may be a feeling:

  - About the changes taking place in oneself or life: insecurity, fear, feeling unsafe. Wanting to go home in this context means wanting to return to a psychological state where everything feels safe and secure.

- "Home" may be a place:

  - Where the person feels more secure and safe, such as bed.

  - Where the person has a sense of belonging.

- "Home" may be a spiritual yearning to:

  - Be in heaven.

  - See relatives who have died.

- "Home" may mean a past time or a place in the past when life was more comfortable:

  - A birthplace

  - A childhood home

  - A family home where the children were raised

  - A recent home

> *Wanting to go home can have many different meanings*

Possible Physical, Medical and Emotional Causes of Wanting to Go Home

- This may be a direct result of physical changes in the brain.

  - She is unable to recognize home as home, due to memory loss or changes in perception.

  - She may be disoriented to time, thinking it is an earlier time in her life when she lived in another place.

- Your relative is feeling fatigued and wants to go to bed. Trying to cope with daily activities can take a tremendous amount of energy. Someone with dementia tires easily and hence is more in need of the comfort of "home."

- She may be depressed.

- She may be expressing grief - sadness, anxiety or anger - about no longer feeling independent and able to make her own decisions.

Strategies to Try for Possible Physical, Medical and Emotional Causes of Wanting to Go Home

- Respond to the emotion being expressed, such as *"Are you feeling scared?"* or *"I know you are feeling lonely."*

- Offer reassurance, *"I will take care of you,"* or *"Don't worry. I will make sure you will have everything you need here."*

- Try to redirect the person's attention with an activity, food, music, dancing, a walk, or other exercise. Often, after a while, the person may forget about wanting to go home.

- Look at a photo album with pictures of your relative's childhood. The chance to reminisce about the past may ease the anxiety and trigger pleasant memories. Avoid asking a lot of direct questions that rely on memory and may cause anxiety. Asking, *"Do you remember this?"* or *"Who is this in the photo?"* can trigger anxiety, feelings of panic or failure and the desire to escape if she cannot remember. Saying *"Oh, look, here we are with Jennifer at the cabin,"* allows the person to engage and respond but does not put her on the spot.

- Try giving your relative a letter to carry that gives her a brief biography describing memorable events from her life. For example, a letter might tell when and where she was born, whom she married, names of her children, etc. For someone who can still read, this can bring comfort and be very reassuring.

- Try to get the person to reminisce about the place or person that is being missed. Wanting to go home is often connected with the desire to see a loved one who is deceased. Don't contradict the person or try to reason about it as this may provoke pointless arguments or may cause unnecessary grieving if the person has forgotten the death.

Possible Environmental Causes of Wanting to Go Home

- Too much activity or noise is causing the person to feel over stimulated. She may feel overwhelmed by the number of people and the noise level and want to leave, sometimes wanting to go home.

- She has recently moved to a new, unfamiliar place.

- Some items in the environment are triggering thoughts of home. A photograph of an old home on the wall, a coat stand with coat and hat, or other objects may cause the person to think of home.

- Wanting to go home may be an emotional response to wanting to be elsewhere. This can occur even if she is in the home where she has lived for a long time.

- She may feel bored. When there is not enough activity, people with dementia often feel uncomfortable and want to return to someplace where she can do things.

Strategies to Try for Possible Environmental Causes of Wanting to Go Home

- Try keeping a diary or log. Write down every time this behavior occurs, recording the following:

  - What time did your relative start focusing on wanting to go home?

  - What happened just before it began?

  - Who was present?

  - What was going on in the environment?

  - Sometimes a pattern may emerge. If the person is particularly insecure or frightened at the same time every day, establish a very specific routine to help build security before wanting to go home begins.

- Remove items from sight that may remind your relative of going home, e.g., hats, coats, a purse, coat rack, etc.

- Consider keeping outdoor clothing out of sight.

- Examine past routines, for events or stresses that may be causing or encouraging wanting to go home.

> *Aaron Schwartz was a policeman who went to work every day at 3:00 pm. Now he becomes agitated and asks to go home at that time. Mrs. Schwartz has learned to take him for a walk or drive a little before 3 PM, which helps them get past that time of day more successfully.*

- Go for a walk or drive. Getting out, even for a short time, can be helpful. Upon returning home, the person with dementia often recognizes it as home.

- Encourage the person to express feelings of loss, fear, or insecurity, which she may be feeling. Often listening to someone with dementia talk about her past can comfort and validate special places, people and experiences in the person's life.

In a Day Center Setting: Suggestions For You to Offer Staff

- Try a reassuring audio or videotaped message from a family member that tells your relative when she will be picked up, and offers her reassurance that her family knows where she is. It might help to tell your relative that she is loved and missed and that family will visit soon. However, for some people, a recording is more confusing than helpful.

> *Judy Davis wanted to go home every day after lunch at the day program. Eventually staff realized that her place at the table faced the wall where hats and coats were hung on hooks. She spent lunchtime looking at the coats which triggered thoughts of home. Changing her seating and placing screens in front of the coats helped with this issue.*

- Ask staff to create a fun and engaging activity for your relative at the time she often wants to go home. It could be a group activity or one-on-one with a volunteer.

- Write a short note that describes what you are doing while your relative is at the day program, e.g., *"I am going to lunch with Ann and will be here to pick you up at 2:30 p.m. Have a nice time. I love you. Your daughter, Joan."* Ask staff to give this note to your relative if she is determined to go home.

- Try a note that instructs your relative to remain at the day center until a specific time when she will be picked up. *"Mother, please stay here until 2:30 PM. when I will come to get you. Love, Jan."*

- Record a short message in a 'talking picture frame', *"Mom, I am at work. I'll pick you up as soon as I'm finished. Have fun at the club!"*

- Ask staff to play your relative's favorite music or bring a favorite CD or iPod with headphones so she can privately enjoy her music.

Sometimes combining several of these strategies, and creating a comforting space for your relative can help her calm down and be able to remain comfortably in the center.

In a Residential Care Setting: Suggestions For You to Offer Staff

- Plan enjoyable things to do with your relative when you visit. Engaging her in a favorite activity can also help to distract her from wanting to go home, even if it is for a short time.

> *When Iris' mom moved to a memory care community, Sally would keep a box of "things to do with mom" in her car. When Sally visited, she would choose one of the activities to do with her mom: looking at an old photo album of family trips, reading post cards and letter from friends, looking at the embroidered linens that her mom had made many years ago.*

- Talk to the staff about staying with your relative the first night of a move into a residential care setting. Moving is often a disorienting, frightening experience and family presence may be helpful.

- Work out a telephone routine with the staff, if a phone call is reassuring. This might involve a daily or occasional call at a time when staff knows you will be home. Sometimes, merely giving your relative your phone number to keep in her pocket can be reassuring.

- Tell the staff how you would like them to respond when your relative asks to go home. Well-meaning staff may say things like *"This is where you live now."* or *"This is your home now."* Hearing these unexpected statements can induce anger, panic or fear. Some people may be comforted hearing *"You will be staying here for a while,"* or *"Your doctor has ordered you to come here for treatment."* Some families are able to respond with words that give the new resident comfort and hope, while other families may find it difficult not to tell their relative anything but the truth. You need to think about what will be most comforting for your relative and then ask staff to use the same words and rationale.

- Try posting a large poster on your relative's wall or door that describes a visit you had together and mentions when you will be coming again. *"Dear Mom, It was wonderful to see you last week and to sing together. I am on a business trip but I will see you soon. Love, Angela."*

- Post an oversized letter on the wall with a photo attached that lets your relative know that she is loved and that her family knows where she is. *"Dear Mom, I am so glad you are staying there. I am playing the violin with the St. Clair Symphony. I will see you soon. Love, your son, Eric."*

- Try having a "visitors' book" available where family and other visitors can write about their visits. Ask staff to reinforce this by reading it with or to the resident. It can help convince her that she is still loved and visited, and is not forgotten.

- Ask staff to involve your relative in an activity that will help her feel useful in some way, (help set the table, sort laundry, greet people, etc.)

- Ask staff to take your relative for a walk outdoors when she is determined to go home. She may be distracted by the sights and conversation and eventually forget about wanting to go home.

- Try looking at personal possessions in the room. *"Mom, I love this afghan. You made this so long ago and I love seeing it here in your room."* Try not to argue or use logic with her if this approach doesn't work.

Strategies to Try When A New Resident Focuses On Wanting To Go Home

- Consider visiting when there is an activity that you can attend with your relative. This may make it easier for both of you.

- Try shortening visits, visiting at another time of day or less frequently. This can help both of you. Keep in mind that lengthy visits may be too difficult; shortening the visit may reduce stress and expectations for new residents.

- Ask staff for assistance in getting your relative engaged in an activity or a meal when it is time for you to leave. After a visit, families may find it easier to leave quietly without saying goodbye, once the resident is involved in the activity.

- Call and check in with staff to see if it is a good day and time to visit. If not, ask if a phone call would be a good idea. If visits are causing intense anxiety and grief when the visitor leaves, families may be asked not to visit for a short while to give the resident time to adjust to her new environment.

Other Considerations for New Residents

- Be aware that some residential care communities have a "no visiting" policy of 2-4 weeks following a move in order "to allow the new resident to adjust to her new home and the staff." This policy can be devastating to a new resident: she can feel abandoned, frightened, agitated and confused. Not having visitors may also hamper and prolong the resident's adjustment. It is important to discuss and question the "no visiting" policy before a person moves into a residential care setting.

- The exception to the "no visiting policy" may be when a new resident becomes increasing agitated and angry about not being able to go home with a visitor. If the new resident becomes so upset after visits that it affects her and disrupts other residents, the family may be asked not to visit for a while. Before accepting this plan:

  - Determine if there are certain visitors who may be more of a trigger for the resident.

  - Consider if fewer visits or visitors may be better.

  - Discuss how long the trial period of not visiting will be.

  - Identify a staff member the family can contact and when this staff member is most available to talk to you.

  - Try short phone calls or write letters assuring your relative that you know where she is living, appreciate the care she is receiving and you will visit soon.

> After Roberto's mom, Maria, moved to the memory care community, her family made a plan to have someone visit every day. When Roberto and his sister Angela visited, they had enjoyable visits even though their mom talked about feeling sad that she could not go back home and live with their dad. When Maria's husband visited, Maria only talked about wanting to go home and became angry at him when he told her she had to stay there. After the visits, Maria's anger continued for several hours, making it difficult for staff and the other residents. Although Maria's husband did not want to stop his visits, he realized that it was too upsetting for them both. During the three weeks he did not visit, he was in daily contact with the staff about how Maria was doing, and Roberto and Angela continued to visit several times a week. Eventually Maria adjusted and accepted her new living environment, making visits enjoyable for everyone.

- Sometimes hearing "I want to go home" causes families to feel so guilty that they consider taking their relative back home for a visit. Staff can be very helpful in deciding if the new resident is ready for outings, especially visiting their previous home. It is important to carefully consider the consequences before doing this:

  - Will the person recognize her home as home?

  - Will she be willing to go back to her new residence after seeing her home?

  - Will visiting her home cause her to be more agitated and hamper her adjustment to the move?

- Family members often think taking their relative home for a visit will bring closure for their relative and help them adjust to the move. Although this may be true for some new residents, a person with dementia may not have the ability to do this. Consider whether seeking closure might be more for the family than for the person with dementia.

- As A LAST RESORT, ask the doctor about medications to calm the person, if the agitated behavior is very frequent and nothing else works.

References

White, L. & Spencer, B. (2006). Moving a Relative with Memory Loss: A Family Caregiver's Guide. Whisp Publications. Whisppub.com

WALKING, PACING, WANDERING OR EXERCISING

WALKING, PACING, WANDERING OR EXERCISING

George has always exercised vigorously, especially when he is stressed or upset about something. Now when he walks the halls or paces, he is labeled a "wanderer."

For decades Marilyn has walked to the grocery store several blocks from her condo. Recently she became disoriented and got lost on the way home. She is now classified as someone who "wanders."

In dementia care, families and professionals often refer to wandering or call people wanderers. Another term that is used in residential care is "elopement." This terminology immediately brings to mind the notion that someone is confused, disoriented and that their behavior is aimless or meaningless. In fact, we now recognize that many times walking behavior has a purpose for the person, if we can figure out what it is.

At the same time, when someone leaves her home or residence and becomes lost, it clearly becomes a safety issue. There are also other risks that need to be evaluated if someone is incessantly walking.

With this behavior, as with all challenging behaviors, it is important to begin with trying to understand underlying causes of the behavior. Walking away or pacing usually, but not always, occurs in the later stages.

Possible Physical, Medical and Emotional Causes of Walking, Pacing, Wandering or Exercising

- Changes in the brain from the dementia can cause:

  - Loss of recognition of her surroundings or no concept of the distance she has walked.

  - A compulsion to keep moving. There can be an increase in restlessness which seems to require constant movement.

  - Depression. Some forms of depression can cause agitation which can, in turn, make a person feel the need to walk around or move constantly.

  - Hallucinations or delusions, sometimes lead to walking behavior as the person is attempting to respond to a false idea or vision.

  - The appearance of wandering when the person needs to go to the bathroom and cannot find it.

- Discomfort from constipation or bowel impaction, especially when seated, may cause a person to want to move.

- Caffeine from coffee, colas, or chocolate may cause restlessness and increase anxiety which can make a person want to keep moving.

- Some medications can also cause these types of reactions. These include medications for asthma, high blood pressure, cold medicines, anti-depressants and anti-psychotics.

- When a person is in pain, she may feel the need to move about. Many older adults have chronic pain from arthritis, from sitting too long or from other chronic conditions. A person with dementia may not talk about or express the pain except through moving about or agitation.

- At night a person may be walking or pacing because she cannot sleep. (See **And Hours to Go Before She Sleeps: Sleep and Sundowning**.)

- The need for exercise may compel a person to walk a great deal.

- Sometimes people are hungry or thirsty and what appears to be aimless walking is actually searching for food or drink. Again, the person may not be able to articulate this need – it is communicated by the behavior.

- Sometimes people forget what they got up to do and may pace around trying to remember.

- A person may feel lonely and be searching for someone.

- Walking may be a response to an emotion such as fear, grief, sadness, or anxiety.

- Boredom can make people restless as they look for something to do.

Strategies to Try for Possible Physical, Medical and Emotional Causes of Walking, Pacing, Wandering or Exercising

- Try keeping a diary or log. Write down every time this behavior occurs and the circumstances surrounding it. (See **Becoming a Detective** section.)

- Have a thorough medical evaluation, particularly if agitation and pacing begin suddenly, to rule out problems with medication(s), infection, dehydration or another underlying medical cause. Also, make sure that your relative has been evaluated for possible depression and that pain is being adequately treated.

- Limit caffeine intake and evaluate whether this reduces agitation and movement. A behavior log is a good way to measure this.

- Pay attention to bathroom habits and make sure this behavior is not a response to constipation or needing to use the bathroom. (See **When You Gotta Go: Helping Your Relative in the Bathroom**.)

- Try to recognize when walking is being caused by a strong emotion and respond to the feeling. It may be a matter of reassuring a scared or anxious person or listening to someone who is sad or grieving and letting them know you are listening. *"Pete, I am going to be with you all day. I'll get you anything you need. We are safe together."*

Possible Environmental Causes of Walking, Pacing, Wandering or Exercising

- Pacing can be a response to being too hot or too cold.

- Curiosity may cause someone to go walking in search of someone to see or something to do.

- An under stimulating environment may cause the person to go looking for stimulation.

- An overstimulating environment (such as one with too much commotion or noise, people arguing, or too many people) can cause someone to try to escape to a quieter place.

- The person may be looking for something that is missing in the environment – access to the outdoors, a particular person, something meaningful to do.

- Your relative may be looking for you or another family member. When there is no one in the room, she may no longer be able to visualize or remember where you are and becomes worried or lonely.

- Triggering items – hats, coats, purses, for example – that remind the person of going somewhere may lead to attempts to leave.

- When the environment is unfamiliar, people often go in search of a familiar place.

- Clothing that is uncomfortable, scratchy, too tight, hot, etc., can cause someone to move around.

Strategies for Possible Environmental Causes of Walking, Pacing, Wandering or Exercising

- Pay attention to when this is happening and think about the environment – is the temperature comfortable for your relative? Is it when you are out of sight? Are there triggering items in sight?

- If your relative can still read, try writing a note on paper or a prominent white board saying where you are. *"Mother, I'm in the basement working at my desk. I'll be back upstairs soon."*

- Try to find things for her to do that can be left out in plain sight and may engage her. This, of course, depends on her abilities, but some ideas are simple jigsaw puzzles, word games, picture books, photo albums, polishing silver, sanding blocks of wood.

- Make sure your relative gets outside regularly, but keep outside garments and reminders out of sight.

- Monitor clothing and shoes for comfort. Sometimes, when people are walking or pacing a great deal of the time, they develop foot problems, blisters or swollen ankles. Watch for these, visit a podiatrist (foot doctor) if necessary, and try to have her elevate her feet a few times during the day if these conditions are present.

♦

Possible Causes Related to Past History

- Your relative may be searching for home or people from the past such as deceased loved ones, usually parents, siblings or a spouse. (For more suggestions, see **There's No Place Like Home**.)

- She may be trying to continue with exercise patterns from the past, such as daily walks or jogging. Also, many people have used exercise as a way to cope with anxiety earlier in their life.

- Memories of a trauma or abuse from the past can recur late in life and may cause the person to feel the need to walk or move from anxiety or fright.

- Some people have had jobs that included a lot of movement or walking, e.g., retired farmers, postmen, policemen or nurses.

- Sometimes a person is trying to recreate an old routine or habit such as leaving for work or picking up the children.

Strategies for Causes Related to Past History

- Again, a diary or log may be helpful in finding a pattern to the walking which can help you think about possible causes.

- Be sure to build exercise into the daily routine if you can. Try to pattern it on your relative's previous exercise routines.

- If there has been a past trauma or history of abuse, try to understand the emotion that is driving the behavior. Could it be fear? Anxiety? Anger? Respond to the emotion as best you can and reassure the person that she is safe.

- If you don't know your relative's past history very well, think about other family members you might ask. Also ask your relative, *"What was your work life like? What did you and dad do after lunch when you retired?"*

- If a routine from the past, such as walking to the mailbox or the corner grocery, seems to be triggering the behavior, try to build a similar routine into the present life, which may satisfy that need.

> *The adult day program staff told Bruce's partner, Gary, that he was trying to leave every day after lunch. Gary realized that that was the time when Bruce would walk down the driveway to the mailbox every day at home. Staff created a mail pick up area in another part of the building for Bruce. Each day after lunch he and a volunteer would walk to pick up the mail and it almost completely ended his attempts to leave the center.*

Possible Causes Related to Being Up or Walking at Night

- Often the person may wake up disoriented and is looking for the bathroom. At night, confusion is often greater because the person is tired, things look different or the light is dim.

- Inactivity during the day can cause wakefulness at night. Sometimes people are sleeping or napping too much during the day.

- The person may have lost the ability to differentiate day and night. Or when she wakes up, she thinks it is time to get up. (See **And Hours to Go Before She Sleeps: Sleep and Sundowning.**)

Strategies for Being Up at Night

- Make sure there is sufficient lighting at night. Nightlights may help. Sometimes leaving the bathroom and hall light or a dim light in the bedroom on is helpful.

- If your relative seems to be getting lost on the way to the bathroom, consider a bedside commode or urinal. This may take some training, but can be helpful in the long run.

- Try to build sufficient exercise into the daily routine so your relative is tired at night.

- If she is mixing up day and night, getting up and dressed at 2:00 am, try giving her a warm beverage, favorite food or involving her in a quiet activity. Sometimes, but not always, the person may go back to bed.

Safety Measures

- Families sometimes have to safety proof the house for nights, hire someone to be a night time companion, or move the person to a more secure part of the house or a secure residential environment. It is not always possible to change this behavior.

- Call 911 if your relative becomes lost.

- Register your relative with the Alzheimer's Association Safe Return program. It is a 24-hour, nationwide emergency response service for individuals with dementia. If someone becomes lost, caregivers can call the 24-hour emergency response line to report it. A community support network including Alzheimer's Association chapters and law enforcement agencies will come together to assist with finding the person who is lost. For information and fees, call 1-888-572-8566 or go online to www. medicalert.org/safereturn.

- Consider a GPS system, which uses global positioning satellites to track the person who is wearing the device. There are a number of systems available. The Alzheimer's Association co-sponsors one called Comfort Zone. For information and fees, call 1-877-259-4850 or go to the website at www.alz.org/comfortzone/shop.asp. Another system is www.projectlifesaver.org.

- Have a current picture of the person available in case she becomes lost. A short videotape of the person may also be helpful. You may wish to share this information with the local police.

- Let neighbors know that your relative has dementia and make sure they have your phone number. They may be very helpful if she leaves home and you don't see her go. Neighbors may also be able to help in a crisis.

- If the person has a tendency to walk away, consider whether it is better not to take her to crowded stores or other public places where you may become distracted and not be able to track her.

- Consider brightly colored outdoor clothing such as a hat, jacket, coat or pants. Reflectors sewn onto sleeves or pant legs may be helpful to police involved in searching for the person. It may also be helpful to have an unwashed piece of clothing available should tracking dogs become involved in searching for the person.

- If your relative uses a cane or a walker, keeping it in the same place may help.

- Remove items from sight that may trigger the desire to go out such as shoes, coats and a purse.

- Try to get the person to rest for a half hour every few hours if she walks a great deal. Raise her feet to prevent swelling. Also make sure she is getting enough to drink and eat to make up for the extra calories burned.

- Slippers should not be worn as they offer no support and contribute to trips and falls. Shoes for indoor and outdoor use must be comfortable and fit snugly with laces or Velcro® fastenings.

- Many safety devices are available in the childproofing section of toy stores, at medical supply stores or online, such as:

  - Child proof door knob covers that prevent the person from turning the door knob. These may be inadvisable for caregivers with arthritic hands.

  - Devices to signal when the outside door opens such as a bell or an alarm system.

  - A simple intercom system or a room monitor so you can hear your relative if you are in another room.

- Be sure to lock the doors at night. Consider installing more complex locks that make it difficult for someone with memory loss to open, such as keyless door lock. Putting a lock in an unfamiliar position such as at the top or bottom of the door sometimes suffices. At the same time, it is important that people be able to exit quickly if there is a fire.

- Never leave your relative locked alone in the house or in a car unsupervised if she becomes anxious or disoriented or is in the later stages of dementia.

- Safety proof the house by keeping medications, cleaning supplies, sharp objects, guns, alcohol and matches locked in cupboards or closets. Disable electric tools.

- Avoid using scatter rugs or area rugs that may lead to falls. Provide safe, uncluttered routes throughout the house for walking.

- Make sure there are handrails on stairs to help prevent falls.

- Keep keys out of sight.

- Remove the car if your relative can no longer drive or is anxious about getting in the car and driving.

- If possible, provide a safe, secured outside area for walking.

Communication and Safety Strategies for Coaxing Your Relative Back to the House

- Fall into step beside her and walk with her. Sometimes singing, holding hands or walking in step can help before you gradually guide her home.

- Stay with her even if you can't get her aimed for home. Just being with her may help her calm down if she is anxious, angry or frightened.

- Always have a cell phone with you so you can call for help if needed.

- Respond to the emotion being expressed: *"Are you feeling scared?"* or *"I know you are feeling lonely."*

- Offer reassurance. For example, *"I will take care of you,"* or *"Don't worry. You will have everything you need here."*

- Try talking about the place the person is trying to reach, if she can identify it. *"I know that house on Prospect St. was one of your favorite places to live."* Sometimes reminiscing about the place is enough to help the person begin to calm down.

- Consider whether this walking is causing problems or if it is just irritating to you. If it is the latter, then the strategies have to do with rethinking how you are responding to the behavior.

Suggestions for Engaging Your Relative in Meaningful Activities at Home

- Consider taking several short walks throughout the day or two or three times a week. If the person is active and physically fit, a walking program may not be enough. Previously enjoyed activities such a swimming, cycling, dancing, aerobic exercises, T'ai Chi and gardening may provide opportunities to be more physically active.

- Go for a drive. Getting out, even for a short time, is often helpful. Upon returning home, she may recognize it as home. Make sure your relative with memory loss is safely buckled in and all doors are locked. Never leave a person unattended in a car. The person may become frightened about being alone, could wander off, release the emergency brake or fiddle with the gear shifts.

- Plan a physical activity at least once during the day. If the person is able to exercise without risk, encourage the person to walk on a treadmill, use a stationary bike, or a rocking chair if the person is frail. Hitting a punching bag, pounding dough or digging in a garden can be effective ways to help someone who is angry or frustrated.

- Ask your relative to help with setting the table, preparing the evening meal, folding the laundry, washing dishes, any activity that will help her feel useful.

- Try to redirect your relative's attention with an activity, food, music, dancing, a walk, or other exercise. Often, after a while, she might forget about wanting to leave.

- Look at a photo album with pictures of her childhood. The chance to reminisce about the past may ease the anxiety and trigger pleasant memories. Avoid asking a lot of direct questions that rely on memory and may cause anxiety.

Other Considerations for Walking, Pacing, Wandering and Exercising

- Understand that if your relative walks away from home and becomes lost, she may not view it that way.

> *Jane Ko was visiting her daughter's house and walked out the door, becoming lost in the neighborhood. After several hours, her daughter, Mina, found her mother sitting on a bench several miles from the house. Mina was frantic, but Jane had no idea she was lost (although she had never been on that street before) or that she had been away for a long time. She just felt she was out for a nice walk. Mina had to restrain herself from scolding her mother.*

- As A LAST RESORT, ask the doctor about medications to calm your relative, if the behavior is very frequent, stressful and nothing else works.

References

Algase, D.L. (1999). Wandering in dementia. Annual Review of Nursing Research, 17: 185-217.

Algase, D.L., Moore D.H., Vandeweerd C., & Gavin-Dreschnack D.J. (2007). Mapping the maze of terms and definitions in dementia-related wandering. Aging & Mental Health, 11: 686–698.

Cohen-Mansfield, J., Werner, P., Culpepper, W.J. & Barkley, D. (1997). Evaluation of an inservice training program on dementia and wandering. Journal of Gerontological Nursing, 23(10): 40-47.

Hiatt, L.G. (1992). Restraint reduction with special emphasis on wandering behavior. Topics in Geriatric Rehabilitation: 8(2):55-77.

Hope R.A., Fairburn CG. (1990). The nature of wandering in dementia—a community based study. International Journal of Geriatric Psychiatry, 5: 239–245.

Rader, J., Doan, J., & Schwab, M. (1985). How to decrease wandering, a form of agenda behavior. Geriatric Nursing, 6(4): 196-99.

Teresi, J. A., Holmes, D., & Ory, M.G. (2000). The therapeutic design of environments for people with dementia: Further reflections and recent findings from the National Institute on Aging Collaborative Studies of Dementia Special Care Units. The Gerontologist, 40(4): 417-421.

WHEN YOU DON'T SEE THINGS THE SAME WAY: PARANOIA, DELUSIONS AND HALLUCINATIONS

WHEN YOU DON'T SEE THINGS THE SAME WAY: PARANOIA, DELUSIONS AND HALLUCINATIONS

Some people with dementia experience paranoia, delusions and hallucinations due to changes in the brain that occur during various stages of their disease. It is important to understand the differences between these symptoms and how they are expressed in different types of dementia.

Definitions and Examples

- **Paranoia**: a blaming belief or suspiciousness that a person with dementia holds onto despite repeated explanations or lack of proof of evidence.

  Mrs. Brown often did not remember where she put her checkbook. In her mind, she always put it in the same place and if it was not there, then someone must have taken it. She would accuse her caregiver of stealing it. Although this was not true, no amount of talking or defending the caregiver would convince Mrs. Brown otherwise.

- **Delusions**: false and irrational beliefs that persist despite all evidence to the contrary.

  Mr. White is positive that he still drives and, in fact, drove to the store this morning, even though he has not actually driven a car for 18 months. Again, no amount of arguing or trying to be logical dissuades him of this delusional belief.

- **Hallucinations**: a perception of something that does not exist. Hallucinations can be visual (seeing something that is not there), auditory (hearing a voice or a sound that does not exist), or tactile (feeling something that is not present).

  After his diagnosis of Lewy Body Dementia (LBD), Larry joked with his wife about the cute little red bugs he saw, but he knew they were not real. As Larry's dementia advanced, he would tell his wife to set another place setting "for the man sitting on the sofa." Even though there was no one there, she found that arguing didn't work and she set the table for three people.

- Hallucinations may occur for people who have Lewy Body Dementia (LDB), vascular dementia, Parkinson's disease (PD), or Alzheimer's disease (AD); however there are significant differences in when they are most likely to occur in the course of the diseases.

  - Visual hallucinations occur in up to 80% of people with LBD, most often beginning in the early stages when the person commonly recognizes that what she sees is not real. As LBD progresses, however, the person cannot distinguish between what is real and what is a hallucination.

  - Hallucinations occur less frequently in people with Alzheimer's disease. If they do occur, it is usually in the later stages, when the person cannot identify what is real and what is not.

- A difference between Lewy Body Dementia (LBD) and Alzheimer's disease (AD), which is noted by some practitioners (Ferman & Dickinson, 2013), is how family members are sometimes misperceived by the individual with the disease. Some people with LBD may believe a family member is a "duplicate or an imposter." A person with AD may misidentify "a relative as another relative, such as mistaking an adult child for a parent."

- In Parkinson's disease the hallucinations are almost always related to the medications used to treat PD; they most frequently occur in low stimulus environments.

Possible Physical, Medical and Emotional Causes of Paranoia, Delusions and Hallucinations

- Sensory deficits due to aging, especially in diminished vision, hearing and taste, can cause these types of behaviors. Cataracts, glaucoma and macular degeneration can also cause changes in depth perception.

- Brain damage due to the progression of Alzheimer's disease or Lewy Body Dementia may contribute to paranoia, delusions or hallucinations in the following ways:

  - The inability to process what the eyes are seeing. When the brain is not accurately processing what the eyes see, objects and people can be misidentified or misinterpreted. This is not a hallucination, but rather a problem with visual perception.

  - Memory loss.

  - Changes in depth perception. For example, a shadow on the floor could be misinterpreted as a hole.

- Psychiatric illness, such as severe depression or bipolar disorder, concurrent with dementia may cause these types of symptoms.

- In frail older adults, physical problems, such as infection, fever, pain or fecal impaction can cause hallucinations and delusions.

- Physical illness such as anemia or respiratory disease, which reduces the amount of oxygen delivered to the brain, may cause these types of symptoms.

- Medications, particularly hormonal medications in combination with antidepressants, or Parkinsons' medications as mentioned above, may contribute to these symptoms.

- Physical trauma from a blow to the head during a fall or other accident can cause hallucinations or delusions.

- Malnutrition or dehydration, resulting in undernourishment of the brain can contribute to these symptoms.

Strategies to Try for Possible Physical, Medical, and Emotional Causes of Paranoia, Delusions and Hallucinations

- Have vision or glasses examined. Visual impairment can easily lead to misinterpretation of the environment.

- Have hearing tested or hearing aids regularly serviced. Diminished hearing also leads to "hearing noises" that are unintelligible, which can lead to auditory hallucinations.

- Seek a medical evaluation to assess for illness, infection, chronic pain or bowel impactions.

- Visually inspect the head and face for bruises or scrapes from unwitnessed falls. If these are present, seek a medical evaluation. This is especially important if there is also a sudden change in the person's level of alertness.

- Request your relative's physician to review all medications, including any over the counter medications that are being taken. Some antipsychotic medications that are prescribed for people with Alzheimer's disease can cause severe side effects for persons with Lewy Body Dementia.

- Seek a psychiatric evaluation of paranoia, delusions, hallucinations, false ideas, or suspiciousness to determine if medication may be helpful. Sometimes medications may be helpful in treating psychotic and delusional symptoms. This should be done under the direct supervision of a physician or psychiatrist.

- Keep in mind that if the hallucination or delusion is not disruptive, unsafe or frightening, it may be better left untreated. If they do not upset the person who is experiencing them, there may be no reason to intervene.

Possible Environmental Causes of Paranoia, Delusions and Hallucinations

- Inadequate lighting, particularly in the evening can cast shadows on objects that may be misidentified.

- Reflections from windows or mirrors may be interpreted as real or a duplicate of what is seen.

- The person is living in a new and unfamiliar environment.

- She does not recognize her home even though it is not a new home.

- Unrecognized or unfamiliar caregivers or other "strangers" may prompt paranoia.

- An established routine has been disrupted, causing the person to feel insecure and a loss of control.

- Removal of items from the person for safety or security reasons, such as guns, knives, money or jewelry, may lead to accusations of stealing.

- An under stimulating environment can lead to hallucinations, particularly in people with Parkinson's disease.

- Misinterpretation of things in the environment due to too much going on, diminished hearing or sight, or not using glasses or hearing aids are common. This misinterpretation seems very normal when we put ourselves in the impaired individual's place.

Mr. Carter was lying in bed without his glasses or hearing aids. A caregiver approached him in the dim light and began pulling down the covers. Mr. Carter screamed, believing he was being attacked. He misunderstood the situation and the intentions due to a combination of his dementia and his sensory losses.

Strategies to Try for Possible Environmental Causes of Paranoia, Delusions and Hallucinations

- Increase lighting in the environment. Try higher wattage bulbs and/or night-lights, as shadows can lead to visual hallucinations.

- Minimize reflections as much as possible by closing curtains or covering mirrors if necessary.

- Put yourself in the physical location of the person having the hallucination or delusion and try to imagine what might be contributing to it.

When Ann's daughter lay in her mother's bed, she realized that the shadows of branches on the walls looked very much like crawling snakes when the wind was blowing. Heavy curtains over the windows took care of this hallucination.

- Change the environment as little as possible. When it is necessary to change the environment:

  - Include familiar objects from the old environment.

  - Whenever possible, have a trusted family member explain the new environment.

  - Give the person a regular and recurring simple task to do in the environment (making her own bed, watering a plant, cleaning tables, etc.).

  - Scan the environment for any shadows or dark objects that may be misinterpreted.

- Be aware of the possibilities of both over and under stimulation. Think about how boring or chaotic the environment is and what you can do to change it.

Communication Tips and Strategies

- If your relative misplaces objects or is suspicious of another person stealing something:

  - Remind her where valuables are stored for safekeeping.

  - Assist her in looking for the misplaced item(s).

  - Give your relative small amounts of money if she is accustomed to having money on her person. This can often give her a sense of control.

  - Do not scold her for losing items or hiding things.

  - If feasible, keep a spare set of items that are frequently missed such as a purse, keys or glasses.

- Learn where her favorite "hiding places" are, and let other caregivers know.

- Encourage your relative to keep the item in the same place.

- Try putting up a sign that identifies where she can put her things: *"Put your purse here."*

- When a person with dementia is upset about something that may be missing, try to discuss her feelings about the lost object.

• Carefully choose your arguments. Arguing or trying to reason with a paranoid or suspicious person often makes the situation worse and can result in increased agitation or anger, creating more stress for everyone.

• Respond to the person's need to talk about a deceased loved one as if the person were still alive. The memory of the person who passed away may be stronger than the memory of his death. Instead of telling the person her father is dead, try saying, *"You must miss your father,"* or *"It sounds like you loved your father very much,"* or *"Tell me about your father."*

> *Mr. Sherba's dog died six months ago and he misses the dog desperately. In a recent conversation with his son, Mr. Sherba angrily accused him of hiding the dog. In response to the accusation his son replied, "You really miss the dog and I do too. She was such good company. I remember how she used to play with the neighbor's dog. Let's go next door and see if the neighbor's dog is in the backyard."*

• Reassure the person that you will look into the "theft" immediately. This may help your relative know that she is being heard and that action is being taken to investigate the missing items.

• Investigate suspicions that may be founded on fact. The person may actually be a victim of robbery, mistreatment or harassment.

• Explain potential or actual misinterpretation: *"That loud noise is an airplane flying overhead."*

• Explain what is happening if your relative is frightened and is able to accept the explanation. *"Your brain is playing tricks on you which makes you see those bugs, even though they are not really there. You are not going crazy."* For some people this approach is very reassuring.

• Listen. Giving the person time and attention without interruption, scolding or disagreeing may alleviate the person's stress or upset.

• Determine if the hallucination is bothering or frightening the person. If not, avoid getting involved in the conversation about whether it is real or not.

> *James was seeing cars and people in the trees outside of his house. He was becoming frustrated that his wife Carol did not see them. Carol learned that it was better not to argue as this only upset both of them. "I decided it was better to listen to what he believed was real and then change the subject."*

- Use familiar distractions such as music, exercise, card playing, conversations with friends, reviewing photo albums, rolling coins, playing with pets, and drawing or sketching. The purpose of the distraction is not to create a great product, but to distract.

- Establish or reinforce a daily routine or parts of a daily routine, such as meal rituals or bedtime rituals. Routines help give structure and a sense of the familiar to the individual who lives in an unfamiliar world. Even a few simple daily routines can help increase a sense of security.

- Use physical touch as reassurance, if the person is willing to accept physical touch. Don't force it upon her. Saying *"I know that you are upset,"* or *"Would it help if I held your hand?"* may reassure her. Non-verbal reassurance such as physical touch or tone of voice often gets through when verbal communications don't.

- Explain to individuals who have frequent contact with your relative that you do not suspect them and that the accusations result from the confused person's inability to assess reality accurately.

- Encourage structured or supervised contact with friends and family who are aware and accepting of confused individuals. Teach family and friends how to respond to a person's hallucinations, delusion or paranoia.

Other Considerations for Paranoia, Delusions and Hallucinations

It is important for caregivers not to take accusations personally. Remember that personality changes can be a result of the illness.

- Keep a diary or log in order to pinpoint whether there are particular times of day, places or people that precede hallucinations, delusions or suspiciousness. If these can be identified, it may be possible to alter the routine and avoid such behaviors, or to anticipate problems and be ready with distractions.

- Changes in vision, hearing and taste are normal as people age. These changes can cause a person without dementia to misinterpret what she is seeing and hearing. Regular check-ups are important to determine what is normal and what might be related to brain changes.

- Everyone can be suspicious at times, some people more than others. The confused individual awakens each day in unfamiliar surroundings, perhaps having forgotten her environment and the trusted people in it. It is understandable that she is suspicious.

- It is important for caregivers not to take accusations personally. Remember that personality changes can be a result of the illness.

- Family and friends who are falsely accused of persecuting or abusing an individual with dementia understandably have great difficulty accepting this behavior, and often choose to avoid the individual. Yet, the individual desperately needs the reassurance that these familiar people can provide.

References

Budson, A.E. & Solomon, P.R. (2011). Memory Loss: A Practical Guide for Clinicians. Elsevier Saunders.

Friedman, J.H. (2013). Making the Connection between Brain & Behavior: Coping with Parkinson's Disease. DemosHealth.

Ferman, T. & Dickinson, D.W. (2013). Early Visual Hallucinations Greatly Increase Odds of LBD over Alzheimer's, Parkinsonism and Related Disorders. http://www.lbda.org/content/early-visual-hallucinations-greatly-increase-odds-lbd-over-alzheimers

AND HOURS TO GO BEFORE WE SLEEP: SLEEP AND SUNDOWNING

AND HOURS TO GO BEFORE WE SLEEP: SLEEP AND SUNDOWNING

Sleep problems are one of the symptoms that are tolerated least well by family caregivers. When care partners are unable to get adequate sleep themselves, night after night, they become high risk candidates for accidents or illness, and their relatives become likely candidates for moving.

Caregivers frequently become so exhausted themselves that they become ill or simply can't continue.

Sleep disturbances in aging people without dementia are common and can include a number of changes: a decrease in deep sleep, more frequent night awakenings, more difficulty falling back to sleep and day time sleepiness.

For people with dementia these sleep disturbances are often more severe. During early stages of a progressive dementia, it is not unusual for people to wake up from naps or in the morning extremely disoriented and to mix up dreams and reality. Sometimes people sleep much longer hours than in the past. Others have much more disrupted sleep. In later stages of the disease, sleep problems may include frequent awakening and mixing up of days and nights. When sleep is disrupted, individuals generally become more disoriented and often it increases their agitation. Clearly this can be an extremely difficult problem for families.

Problems with sleeping or late evening agitation are often a stage in dementia that eventually passes. Many people with Alzheimer's begin sleeping more during the later stages of the illness.

> *Amanda Boyer appeared exhausted. Her mother who had Alzheimer's disease lived with her and was sleeping less and less at night. Sometimes she would be roaming the house at 2:00 am, opening closets and cupboards and moving things around. Amanda worried that she might injure herself or walk out of the house. Other nights her mom would get dressed in the middle of the night thinking it was morning. Amanda was up every night trying to get her mother back to bed. Sometimes she succeeded but often she herself could not get to sleep again. During the day her mother would fall asleep in her recliner and would wake up groggy and confused, saying things that made no sense. Amanda was at her wit's end.*

Possible Physical, Medical and Emotional Causes of Sleep Problems

- Brain changes related to progressive dementia may include a disruption in normal day/night rhythms and the loss of ability to fall into a deep sleep.

- Sleep disorders, including sleep apnea, restless leg syndrome, and REM sleep behavior disorder become more common as people age:

  - **Obstructive sleep apnea (OSA)**, "a condition in which the flow of air pauses or decreases during breathing while you are asleep because the airway has become narrowed, blocked, or floppy."
    http://www.nlm.nih.gov/medlineplus/ency/article/000811.htm

Other Possible Causes of Sleep Problems

- Poor sleep habits can cause sleep difficulties. Good sleep habits (sometimes called sleep hygiene) include going to bed and getting up at the same time every day, as well as some of the points listed below.

- The person is in bed too long at night

- The person is napping too long during the day.

- Being overly tired can make it hard for her to relax or calm down.

- Not exercising or exercising too close to bedtime can both contribute to sleep problems.

- Watching television in bed or near bedtime can cause an increase in wakefulness or sometimes lead to agitation.

- Caffeine, alcohol, and cigarettes can all contribute to sleep disruptions.

- Eating too much too late in the evening can affect the ability to sleep.

- Hunger can also make it hard to sleep.

- Discussing the next day the night before may trigger a wakeful response from your relative. Some people with dementia become anxious about upcoming events and will stay awake much of the night worrying about it.

- Feeling tense for a known or unknown reason can interfere with sleep.

- Agitation from an upsetting situation, such as an argument with a family member or an upsetting scene on television, can make it difficult to settle down to sleep.

Strategies to Try for Other Possible Causes of Sleep Problems

- Try experimenting with the amount of time in bed, bedtimes and wake up times. Try getting your relative up at an earlier hour or keeping her up later until she is tired. Some people require only 6-8 hours of sleep. Many older adults require less sleep than in the past. Keep a log for a week or so to note what works best.

- Have your relative spend less time in bed if she is in bed more than 8 hours. Once you've found an optimal amount of time in bed, keep bedtimes and getting up times consistent.

- Continue bedtime rituals from the past (e.g., a glass of milk before bed, or music on the radio at bedtime).

- Try to prevent daytime napping, unless the person seems very fatigued in the evening hours. Then try a short rest or nap after lunch. Setting the clock for a timed nap may help.

- Make sure the person is getting adequate exercise. Try to take one or two vigorous walks a day.

- Cut down on or eliminate caffeine (coffee, tea, colas, chocolate) during the day. Try only decaffeinated beverages. If your relative does drink caffeinated beverages, limit them to the morning, then switch to decaffeinated after lunch.

- Cut down on or eliminate alcohol intake. Discuss the effects of alcohol and medications being taken with the doctor or pharmacist. Non-alcoholic beer or wine might be a good substitute.

- Make sure she is not hungry at night. Try a light snack before bed or during the night. Some herbal teas may have a calming effect. Warm milk often helps promote sleep. At the same time, don't eat large meals late at night. Uninterrupted sleep is more likely when the stomach is not full.

- If bathing is upsetting to your relative, avoid it late in the day.

- If bathing is relaxing to her or if this has been a longstanding habit, try a warm evening bath or shower before bed.

- Avoid laying clothes out for the next day or talking about the next day's activities. This may be confusing and give her a "wake-up" signal.

- Allow her to sleep on a couch or in armchair, if she is refusing to get into bed.

- Give your relative a backrub or massage her legs at bedtime or during nighttime wakefulness to help relax her.

- Try softly playing the radio or a favorite CD beside the bed.

- Gently remind your relative that it is dark out and time for sleeping.

Allowing Your Relative to be Up at Night

Sometimes none of these strategies work well and the individual with dementia is up and down at night on a regular basis. Families handle this in different ways. As mentioned earlier, this can be a major reason for moving the person into residential care. But some families are able to handle sleep disruptions when there is a safe environment and multiple caregivers available.

- It may be helpful for caregivers to learn meditation or relaxation techniques to help themselves fall back asleep.

- Hire a nighttime companion or work out shifts so that the primary caregiver can get sleep.

Randall was up and down repeatedly at night going to the bathroom. Sometimes he fell back asleep but often he didn't. His wife, Tammy, was exhausted but had a number of family members and friends offering to help. She was able to enlist them to sign up for every other night shifts so that she could get a full night's sleep every other night. This strategy worked for Tammy and her family for a number of months. Eventually Tammy needed more sleep than she was able to get every other night and Randall moved to a memory care community.

- Consider allowing your relative to be up at night, if this can be accomplished safely and without disrupting household routines.

- If the care partner and the family member with dementia are sleeping in separate rooms, try using a room monitor to alert the caregiver of any unusual sounds or activities. People in the early stages of dementia may be comforted to know that their caregiver can hear them if they need help.

Safety Considerations

Make the house, or an area of the house, safe for the person to walk around alone at night. Safety proofing a house for safe night walking might include:

- Securing the stairs

- Installing special locks or alarms on doors to the outside

- Installing door or motion sensors

- Blocking off the kitchen

- Locking up dangerous items, such as medications, alcohol, cleansers, guns, knives, etc.

- Making sure windows are locked

Sundowning

There is no consistent definition for sundowning but it generally refers to increased agitation, restlessness and confusion in the late afternoon, early evening or at night, when the sun is going down. Below are the most often recommended strategies for dealing with increased activity or agitation late in the day or early evening:

- Keep a log to determine if sundowning occurs at approximately the same time of the day or under certain conditions, such as too much activity or people in the environment. (See **Becoming a Detective** section.)

- Try to involve your relative in an activity: put on music; give the person something to hold, feel, or fiddle with; go for a walk; try a craft activity; turn on the television (but only if it is something soothing).

- Try closing blinds or curtains to shut out the darkness.

- Turn on lots of lights to brighten the atmosphere and combat shadows.

- Try to be rested for better coping at the most agitated time of day.

- Try to minimize noise, confusion, and the number of people around during the most agitated time of day.

- Try a rocking chair.

- Increase daytime exercise.

- Create soothing evening rituals: a quiet room with bright light, soothing music, gentle massage, or something interesting to do.

- Recreate past evening rituals if they were comforting to your relative (a favorite TV show, watching a movie, a warm bath, etc.)

References

McCurry, S.M., Reynolds III, C.F., Ancoli-Israel, S., Teri, L., & Vitiello, M. V. (2000). Treatment of sleep disturbance in Alzheimer's disease. Sleep Medicine Reviews, 4(6), 603-628.

McCurry, S. M., Gibbons, L. E., Logsdon, R. G., Vitiello, M., & Teri, L. (2003). Training caregivers to change the sleep hygiene practices of patients with dementia: The NITE-AD Project. Journal of the American Geriatrics Society, 51(10), 1455-1460.

http://www.ninds.nih.gov/disorders/restless_legs/detail_restless_legs.htm

http://www.nlm.nih.gov/medlineplus/ency/article/000811.htm

http://www.mayoclinic.org/rem-sleep-behavior-disorder/

http://sleepfoundation.org/sleep-disorders-problems/alzheimers-disease-and-sleep

PHYSICAL INTIMACY AND SEXUAL BEHAVIOR

PHYSICAL INTIMACY AND SEXUAL BEHAVIOR

Of all the behavior changes that can be caused by dementia, the changes in intimacy and sexual expression are the least talked about by care partners. Care partners often say they are: too embarrassed to talk about it; feel the lack of interest in sex is "my fault;" or do not know how to respond to their partner who expresses a continuing or increased need for sex.

Physical intimacy is a complex issue in dementia care. For spouses or partners – of the same sex or opposite sex – physical intimacy sometimes becomes an issue that is emotionally painful and causes great tension as the disease progresses. A care partner may no longer wish to engage in sexual activity, but the person with the disease may still be interested or becomes more frequently or easily aroused. At other times the person with the disease completely loses interest in a sexual relationship while the care partner may still be interested. This is very individual and dependent on many factors, including the type of dementia, one's personality, previous relationship and other medical conditions.

Physical intimacy is unique to the person and the couple. Support groups, medical appointments and counseling sessions do not always address intimacy issues, but it is frequently on care partners' minds. Health care professionals often have not been trained to talk about or ask about intimacy or sexual issues. It may be up to you to raise the issue and ask for help.

A few suggestions are given below, followed by some excellent resources for those who need or wish for additional information.

Physical intimacy and sexual behaviors are complex issues in dementia care.

What is Normal?

Sexual behavior is more difficult to generalize about than some other behaviors. What is normal for one individual or couple may be seen as deviant by others. If an individual has always been flirtatious and now has dementia and is even more flirtatious, is that inappropriate behavior or just a continuation of her previous personality? If a couple has enjoyed a robust sex life that is now complicated by the person with dementia not recognizing her partner, is it still ethical to enjoy sex? If two otherwise married individuals with dementia in assisted living develop an intimate relationship, is that normal or inappropriate? If an individual with dementia shows interest for the first time in a homosexual relationship, is that inappropriate?

There are no clear or right answers to these questions. So much depends on the values, beliefs, comfort level and history of those who are involved in the situation.

While many of the most difficult situations for care partners come from hypersexual or disinhibited behaviors, these are in fact quite rare. There is no agreed upon definition of hypersexuality, but most definitions discuss it as a dysfunctional obsession with sexual urges, behaviors or fantasies. It is more common in men than women. Disinhibition is a term for "socially inappropriate" behaviors, which could include undressing or fondling oneself or others in public, for example. Loss of interest in sex or intimacy in a person with dementia is much more common.

Physical Intimacy Issues for Care Partners

- Probably the most common issue is when a partner with dementia wants to continue an active sex life when you are no longer comfortable with it. It appears to be most common with female caregivers and male partners. One research study (Hayes et al., 2009) found that men were comfortable continuing the sexual relationship longer than women caregivers, who often described "feeling like I'm his mother." Losing a partner who can no longer fully exchange thoughts and feelings can be devastating and is frequently not talked about.

- Another issue is when a caregiver wants to continue the sexual relationship after a partner with dementia has lost interest or ability. As the brain changes with dementia, loss of interest in sexuality and increasing inability to express feelings of love are common. The person with dementia sometimes forgets the sequence or steps involved in sexual expression. Also, there is some evidence that erectile dysfunction is very common among men with Alzheimer's disease (Davies et al., 1998).

- Many caregivers and their partners feel comforted by continuing the sexual relationship for some time. This is often an activity where a person with dementia can continue to be successful and feel like an equal partner.

Strategies When Physical Intimacy is Difficult with Your Partner

- Find someone to talk to about this very difficult issue. It could be a friend, counselor, physician, religious mentor, or family member. While there may be no clear solution, sharing your feelings about it may be helpful.

- If your partner continues to want physical intimacy longer than you do, try to find other ways of being intimate. This might include showering together, cuddling, or other physical demonstrations of affection that exclude intercourse. Be aware that some of these ways of showing your affection may arouse your relative or be misinterpreted as an invitation for sex.

- Some caregivers decide to sleep in a different room as one way to address this issue.

> *Debby and Paul had been together for 25 years when Paul developed dementia. They had always had a very satisfying sex life. Debby began to feel uncomfortable about sex as Paul was getting more confused. Sometimes she felt like she was in a mothering role rather than an intimate partner, and sometimes he was confused about who she was. When she tried to discourage his advances, he felt rejected and sometimes became angry. She began sleeping in another room, telling him that she slept better in her own room. To help both of them with this transition, she would "tuck him in," wait until he went to sleep and then go to sleep in her bedroom.*

- If you want physical intimacy longer than your partner with dementia, pay attention to your partner's emotional reactions. There may come a time when she does not understand what is happening and may feel violated.

Possible Physical, Medical and Emotional Causes of Hypersexuality and Disinhibition

- Hypersexuality is more common in some forms of dementia than others, notably Frontotemporal dementia. In this case, it is due to particular changes in the brain. It appears to be more common in men.

- In rare instances, there are medications that may increase sexual interest and behaviors.

- A preoccupation with sex could be an unspoken desire for emotional intimacy. For some people physical intimacy is the time when they have experienced a sense of validation and self-worth. They may be seeking this validation even though it may feel to the care partner like an insistent desire for sex.

- Disinhibited behaviors can occur from changes in the brain or from misunderstanding a situation or both.

> *When Jack moved to a memory care unit, his wife was mortified to learn that he propositioned young nursing assistants. He was often found masturbating as he sat in the common area. When she visited, his wife would scold and lecture him, but his behaviors continued. Most of the propositions to staff occurred when they were helping Jack with personal care. They learned that he did not understand why young women were touching his private areas. Staff began asking him to clean his own genitals, instead of them doing it. The staff were trained how to respond to his overtures kindly but firmly and he accepted their rejections with good humor. They also learned to identify the signs that Jack was getting ready to masturbate and would move him to a private room. While the behaviors did not go away, they were managed with respect.*

- Seeing someone in tight pants or a low cut blouse may be misinterpreted as an invitation to touch or fondle.

> *When Susan returned home, her husband's caregiver reported that she could no longer work with Richard because he had made "unwanted sexual advances" towards her. Susan was shocked to hear this because the caregiver had been working with Richard for nearly a year and nothing like this had ever happened. When Susan saw that the caregiver's t-shirt said "Love Me" on it, she immediately understood why her husband acted in this way. Susan instructed the caregiver not to wear any clothing that had words or pictures on it that Richard could misinterpret.*

- Sometimes we misinterpret actions that may simply be due to memory loss.

> *Andrew sometimes left his belt or zipper undone in public. His daughter was mortified and thought he might be making sexual advances as he sometimes made suggestive comments. However, it became clear when the family paid attention that Andrew simply forgot to zip up his pants after visiting the bathroom.*

- Overstimulating television, music or conversation may be misunderstood or misinterpreted.

Strategies for Hypersexuality and Disinhibition

- Pay attention to possible triggers of the behavior. Keeping a log may be helpful. Notice if it occurs during a particular activity or in response to someone in the environment as in the case study above. Use your observations to guide your strategies.

- Try distraction or redirection. For some people this works for a while.

- Sometimes behavior modification works for people who are making lewd comments or gestures. This involves reinforcing positive behaviors, being clear about saying "no" and not allowing the behavior to get extra attention.

- Talk with your relative's doctor about the behaviors. Ask for a review of medications or health issues that could be impacting the behaviors. If behavioral interventions such as those suggested don't work, ask your doctor for medications that can help with the behavior. Some anti-depressant medications decrease the desire for sexual activity and generally have fewer side effects than other options, such as hormonal treatments or antipsychotic medications which are sometimes used.

- Try to give your relative privacy as needed if masturbation is an issue.

- If you think the behavior has more to do with emotional intimacy needs than sexual needs, you could try more physical contact such as hugging, holding hands, etc., and more verbal reassurance. *"You are very important to me, David, and I am here for you."*

Other Considerations

This is a very cursory discussion for an extremely complex and personal topic. We felt the need to acknowledge it, and for care partners to know that intimacy and sexuality issues are rarely talked about. We encourage you to explore the resources below and to find someone with whom you can talk about intimacy and sexuality issues.

Resources

Sexuality & Dementia: Compassionate & Practical Strategies for Dealing with Unexpected or Inappropriate Behaviors, Douglas Wornell, MD, DemosHealth, 2014. This book is written for families and professionals and includes chapters on intimacy, the neurobiology of sex and dementia, sexuality in long-term care, and treatment options.

Coping with Changes in Your Intimate Relations, Family Caregiver Alliance http://caregiver.org/sexuality-and-dementia

Fact Sheet on Sex and Dementia, Alzheimer's Society, UK http://www.alzheimers.org.uk/site/scripts/download_info.php?fileID=1801

National Resource Center on LGBT Aging, http://www.lgbtagingcenter.org/index.cfm Includes links to pamphlets on the following:
Providing Quality Care to LGBT Clients with Dementia
LGBT Caregiver Concerns (Alzheimer's)
Legal Plans (Alzheimer's)

References

Davies, H.D., Zeiss, A.m., Shea, E.A., & Tinklenbert, J.R. (1998). Sexuality and intimacy in Alzheimer's patients and their partners, Sexuality and Disability, 16(3): 193-203.

Hayes, J., Boylstein, C. & Zimmerman, M.K. (2009). Living and loving with dementia: Negotiating spousal and caregiver identity through narrative, Journal of Aging Studies, 23: 48-59.

Tucker, I. (2010). Management of inappropriate sexual behaviors in dementia: a literature review, International Psychogeriatrics, 22(5): 683-692.

Wornell, D. (2014). Sexuality & Dementia: Compassionate & Practical Strategies for Dealing with Unexpected or Inappropriate Behaviors, Demos Medical Publishing.

GLOSSARY

GLOSSARY

Care partners often tell us they do not understand the meaning of some of the terms their relative's doctor or other health care professionals use to describe a condition or a symptom. The following list includes some of the most common terms you may hear.

Activities of Daily Living (ADLs): A term used in health care to describe the tasks or activities that are part of our daily life. Usually ADLs include things to do with personal care – dressing, eating, bathing, going to the toilet, and functional mobility while doing these activities. Instrumental Activities of Daily Living (IADLs) include driving, handling finances, managing medications, cooking, doing laundry. It is usually in the realm of IADLs where people first have difficulty.

Agnosia: The failure to recognize familiar objects or people. The person's brain is no longer connecting what the object looks like with its function. If there is aphasia as well, the name of the object may no longer connect in the person's mind. If you ask your relative to pick up the fork and she just stares at it, that may be agnosia or aphasia or both.

Alzheimer's disease: The most common cause of progressive dementia. It is estimated that between 50-75% of those with dementia have Alzheimer's disease. It becomes more prevalent and risk increases with each decade of age. Early onset Alzheimer's is a term given to people who are diagnosed under age 60; early onset is rare. The hallmark of Alzheimer's disease is memory loss, which is nearly always the first symptom. It begins gradually and subtly and is progressive. The speed of progression varies greatly from individual to individual, though symptoms increase in severity over time. Many other symptoms occur during the progression of Alzheimer's disease, including word-finding, difficulty with judgment and decision-making, problem-solving and reasoning abilities; in later stages people often develop difficulty with mobility, incontinence and other physical problems.

Apathy: The lack of a feeling, emotion, interest or concern. Apathy can be caused by depression, changes in the brain due to dementia, or reactions to medications.

Aphasia: "An impairment of language, affecting the production or comprehension of speech and the ability to read or write." People with aphasia caused by dementia or stroke have difficulty expressing what they want to say. It can also affect their ability to understand what you say. National Aphasia Association. http://www.aphasia.org.

Apraxia: The inability to perform a physical task, even though coordination and strength are not affected. Difficulty getting in or out of a car may be an example of apraxia. Even though the muscles are working, the brain patterns have been interrupted in ways that make it impossible for the person to follow through with the action.

Antipsychotics: Medications that are used to try to decrease hallucinations, delusions, paranoia and anxiety. While they are sometimes very helpful and necessary, they are powerful drugs that can have many side effects.

Caregiver / Care Partner: Terms used to describe the person or people who assist with the care of another individual. Care partner is a term preferred by many because it implies that the person with dementia and the family member or non-relative are partners in the journey and that the person with dementia has some say in what happens. Caregiver implies that the family member does all the giving and the person with dementia does all the receiving.

Circumlocution: Using a description of an object rather than the object's name, because the person can't remember the word. For example she might say "That thing that you sit on," instead of "That chair."

Confabulation: Making up facts or stories to fill in the gaps in memory. This is not usually a conscious decision, but is something the person's brain does to try to make sense of a world that is not making sense anymore.

Delusions: False and irrational beliefs that persist despite all evidence to the contrary.

Delirium: Sudden or rapid onset of confusion and loss of awareness. When a sudden change in cognitive abilities or level of confusion occurs, have your relative checked for delirium which is most often caused by an acute medical condition such as infection.

Dementia: An "umbrella" term used to describe a collection of symptoms rather than the name of a specific disease. Dementia can be caused by numerous treatable conditions including urinary tract infection, side effect of medications, vitamin deficiencies, dehydration, etc. Dementia can also be caused by one or more brain disorders that create difficulty in various cognitive abilities which may include memory, attention, problem-solving, language, motivation, social behavior, visual and spatial recognition. Eventually dementia causes people to have difficulty with daily functioning if the cause is a progressive neurological disease. It is important to understand that there are more than 80 identified diseases that can cause these changes in the brain. Another, recently recognized term for dementia is Major Neurocognitive Disorder.

Disinhibition: A term for "socially inappropriate" behaviors, which could include undressing, or fondling oneself or others in public, for example.

Dyskinesia: An abnormal jerking movement that a person is not able to control. An example is uncontrolled mouth movements – sticking one's tongue in and out or making chewing movements. Dyskinesia can be caused by brain changes or can be a side effect of medications.

Edema: Swelling, most commonly in the feet or ankles.

Frontotemporal dementias (FTD): Progressive neurological disorders that primarily affect the frontal and temporal lobes of the brain (forehead and side of head). They tend to occur in younger people, with the majority of cases showing up in individuals between 45 and 65. There are several forms of FTD, including one that is characterized primarily by language problems (aphasia) and another that is characterized by significant changes in behavior and personality.

Hallucination: A perception of something that does not exist. Hallucinations can be visual (seeing something that is not there), auditory (hearing a voice or a sound that does not exist), or tactile (feeling something that is not present).

Hypersexuality: A dysfunctional obsession with sexual urges, behaviors or fantasies. It is more common in men than women.

Incontinence (can be fecal incontinence or urinary incontinence): The inability to hold onto one's urine or feces. There are many causes, but it is common for people to become incontinent in the later stages of dementia.

Lewy Body disease (LBD): Considered by some to be the second most common cause of progressive dementia. Early symptoms often include some Parkinsonian symptoms (such as those listed under Parkinson's disease (PD) below), hallucinations, large fluctuations from day to day in alertness and functioning, impairment in visuospatial abilities, and changes in decision-making and judgment. Lewy Body dementia and

Parkinson's with dementia appear to have some overlapping features. Some physicians and researchers say that if the movement problems come first, then it is Parkinson's disease; if the cognitive changes come first, then it is Lewy Body dementia. Individuals with LBD often have increased sensitivity to some medications.

Mild Cognitive Impairment (MCI) or Mild Neurocognitive Disorder: Relatively recent terminology used to describe people with mild cognitive changes who are not functionally impaired enough to meet the criteria for dementia. MCI is categorized according to whether memory is the main problem (amnestic MCI) or some other cognitive domain, such as language, judgment or decision-making difficulties (non-amnestic MCI).

Neuropathy: "Peripheral neuropathy, a result of damage to the peripheral nerves, often causes weakness, numbness and pain, usually in the hands and feet. It can also affect other areas of the body." http://www.mayoclinic.org/diseases-conditions/peripheral-neuropathy/basics/definition/con-20019948

Paranoia: A blaming belief or suspiciousness that a person with dementia holds onto despite repeated explanations or lack of proof of evidence.

Parkinson's disease (PD): A progressive neurological disease, typically characterized by changes in motor functions, such as tremor, mobility problems, slowness and lack of facial expression. Eventually many people who have PD experience cognitive changes and are considered to have Parkinson's with dementia.

Perseveration: "Continual involuntary repetition of a mental act usually exhibited by speech or by some other form of overt behavior." Merriam-Webster online. m-w.com

Psychosis/Psychotic: "Psychosis occurs when a person loses contact with reality. The person may: Have false beliefs about what is taking place, or who one is (delusions): See or hear things that are not there (hallucinations)." http://www.nlm.nih.gov/medlineplus

Psychotropic Medications: Medications prescribed for psychiatric symptoms. Categories of psychotropic meds include antipsychotics, anti-depressants, anti-anxiety agents and mood stabilizers.

REM (Rapid Eye Movement) sleep behavior disorder: "A sleep disorder in which you appear to physically act out vivid, often unpleasant dreams with abnormal vocal sounds and movements during rapid eye movement (REM) sleep." REM sleep behavior disorder is common in individuals with Parkinson's disease and Lewy Body Dementia, particularly in men. http://www.mayoclinic.org/rem-sleep-behavior-disorder/

Restless leg syndrome (RLS): "A neurological disorder characterized by throbbing, pulling, creeping, or other unpleasant sensations in the legs and an uncontrollable, and sometimes overwhelming, urge to move them. Symptoms occur primarily at night when a person is relaxing or at rest and can increase in severity during the night." RLS is more common in women. http://www.ninds.nih.gov/disorders/restless_legs/detail_restless_legs.htm

Sleep apnea: Obstructive sleep apnea (OSA), "a condition in which the flow of air pauses or decreases during breathing while you are asleep because the airway has become narrowed, blocked, or floppy." http://www.nlm.nih.gov/medlineplus/ency/article/000811.htm

Subjective memory complaints: A recently introduced term to describe the condition where individuals experience memory or cognitive changes in themselves that are too subtle to be picked up by diagnostic testing. Current research cannot tell us whether subjective memory complaints are a good predictor of dementia in the future.

Sundowning: No consistent definition for sundowning, but it generally refers to increased agitation, restlessness and confusion in the late afternoon, early evening or at night, when the sun is going down.

UTI (Urinary Tract Infection): A common cause of sudden change in behavior, confusion level, or an increase in apathy. In some people, common symptoms of a UTI or other infection are those just stated rather than the physical changes, such as fever or pain, that we might expect. Dark colored, strong smelling urine may be signs of a UTI. Whenever you see a sudden change in behavior or level of consciousness contact your relative's doctor immediately.

Vascular dementia: Cognitive impairment that results from changes in the blood vessels of the brain – cerebrovascular disease. This type of disease results in multiple small strokes in the brain that cause dementia symptoms. Changes in attention, judgment and decision-making, and speed of thinking are often present. Vascular dementia is often present with Alzheimer's disease. The major risk factors for vascular dementia are hypertension, heart disease, smoking and diabetes. Treatment involves controlling risk factors as much as possible.

RESOURCE LIST FOR PEOPLE WITH DEMENTIA, CARE PARTNERS AND HEALTH CARE PROFESSIONALS

RESOURCE LIST FOR PEOPLE WITH DEMENTIA, CARE PARTNERS AND HEALTH CARE PROFESSIONALS

The rapidly growing number of resources for people with memory loss, families and professionals, makes it impossible to list all the books, newsletters, videos and websites, but here is a sampling of our favorites. Some titles may be available electronically.

Websites

General information about types of dementia, available resources, educational programs and tips for caring for someone with dementia can be found on the following websites.

www.alz.org

The Alzheimer's Association provides educational programs, support groups, and publications for people with memory loss and family caregivers. Many chapters offer seminars and conferences for professionals. Contact information for local chapters is also posted on the website.

www.alzfdn.org

The Alzheimer's Foundation of America has educational information for the public and for caregivers, online support groups, advice from experts, and links to clinical trials and more.

www.lbda.org

The Lewy Body Dementia Association helps families and professionals better understand this often misunderstood disease. Diagnosing LBD, living with LBD, caring for a person with Lewy Body dementia, as well as blogs are posted on this website.

www.theaftd.org

The Association for Frontotemporal Degeneration provides factual information for newly diagnosed persons, caregiver tips and resources related to frontotemporal dementias (FTD).

www.caregiver.org

Family Caregiver Alliance offers fact sheets, caregiver tip sheets as well as resources by state.

www.caregiveraction.org

Caregiver Action Network provides resources, peer support and advocacy opportunities.

www.eldercare.gov/Eldercare.NET/Public/Index.aspx

Eldercare Locator is a government funded website to help caregivers and professionals locate referral agencies anywhere in the US.

www.nia.nih.gov/alzheimers

Alzheimer's Disease Education and Referral (ADEAR) Center is a service of the National Institute on Aging. ADEAR provides free publications, fact sheets, information on clinical trials, resources and tips for people with dementia, health care providers and family caregivers.

www.nia.nih.gov/alzheimers/alzheimers-disease-research-centers

The National Institute on Aging funds Alzheimer's Disease Centers across the United States. Many of these centers have extensive educational materials, videos, information on research updates and how to participate in clinical trials.

Video Resources

HBO Alzheimer's Project

www.hbo.com/alzheimers/caregivers.html

The Alzheimer's Project is a four-part series: ***The Memory Loss Tapes*** features seven people with dementia; ***Momentum in Science*** takes a look at cutting edge research into Alzheimer's disease; ***"Grandpa, Do You Know Who I Am?"*** by Maria Shriver, takes a look at Alzheimer's from a child's perspective; and ***Caregivers*** features families at different stages of caregiving.

Terra Nova Films

www.terranova.org

Offers a wide selection of videos on aging and other topics, including dementia. Videos can be rented or purchased.

You Tube

www.YouTube.com

A variety of educational videos made by family caregivers, educators and professional videographers are available for viewing. Begin by inserting Dementia, Alzheimer's documentaries, Alzheimer's disease (or another type of dementia), Alzheimer's caregiver, caregiver tips, etc., in the search box.

Personal Reflections by People with Memory Loss

A Look Inside Alzheimer's: I Know Who I am Today, But What About Tomorrow? Marjorie Allen, Susan Dublin, Patricia Kimmerly, DemosHealth, 2013. Two of the authors have Alzheimer's disease, and one is a caregiver. All talk about their experiences with dementia.

Alzheimer's from the Inside Out, Richard Taylor, Baltimore, MD: Health Professions Press, 2007. A clinical psychologist writes about his confusion, frustration, and his day-to-day experiences related to having Alzheimer's.

Living with Dementia: Resources for Living Well, University of Waterloo, Waterloo, Ontario, Canada, Murray Alzheimer's and Research Program (MARP). http://www.livingwithdementia.uwaterloo.ca A website that offers information and resources to help "enable those newly diagnosed with dementia and their families to have the necessary information to live well and help prepare for the road ahead." There is also a guide series for care partners. uwaterloo.ca/murray-alzheimer-research-and-education-program/persons-living-dementia

Dancing with Dementia, Christine Bryden, Jessica Kingsley Publishers, 2005. Christine chronicles her experiences of living with early onset dementia at the age of 46.

Life In the Balance: A Physician's Memoir of Life, Love and Loss with Parkinson's Disease and Dementia, Thomas Graboys, Sterling Publishers, 2008. A doctor turned patient recounts his life with a movement and memory disorder.

My Journey Into Alzheimer's Disease: Helpful Insights for Family and Friends, Robert Davis (with help from his wife Betty), Tyndale House, 1989. One of the first memoirs, this book includes two chapters we find especially helpful: "The abnormal changes so far" and "Spiritual changes that bring confusion."

On Pluto: Inside the Mind of Alzheimer's, Greg O'Brien, Codfish Press, 2014. An award winning journalist describes his experience with early onset Alzheimer's. He says it's a book about living with Alzheimer's, not dying of it.

Partial View: An Alzheimer's Journal, Cary Henderson, Southern Methodist Press, 1998. This book is a photo essay and taped reflections about a professor's experience with Alzheimer's.

The Shapes of Memory Loss: Stories, Poems and Essays from the University of Michigan Medical School and Health System, Nan Barbas, Laura Rice-Oeschger, Cassie Starback, M Publishing, University of Michigan, 2013. This is a compilation of writing by individuals with memory loss, care partners, and health professionals.

You are Not Alone: Poems of Hope and Faith, Lon Cole, Brown and Sons Publishing, 2013. A collection of inspirational poems describes how the author deals with life and dementia.

Young Hope: The Broken Road, Tracy Mobley, Outskirts Press, 2007. The author describes her experience of having early onset Alzheimer's disease.

Window of Opportunity: Living with the Reality of Parkinson's and the Threat of Dementia, Kirk Hall, North Slope Publications, 2014. The author writes this personal account of turning cognitive impairment associated with Parkinson's disease into an opportunity to help others.

Newsletters, Booklets and Books Written for People with Memory Loss

Help and Hope for Persons Diagnosed with Alzheimer's disease and related disorders, Alzheimer's Association, Northern California and Northern Nevada. A 13 page booklet provides basic information on getting a diagnosis, living with memory loss, and taking care of yourself. www.alz.org/norcal/documents/06-2011_earlystage_helpandhopehandbook.pdf

Insight is an online quarterly newsletter written for and by people with dementia published by The Alzheimer's Society of British Columbia. Subscribe online to receive Insight by email or via post mail. www.alzheimerbc.org

Living with Mild Cognitive Impairment, Nicole Anderson, Kelly Murphy, and Angela Troyer, Oxford University Press, 2012. Sections in this book address MCI: what it is, how it is diagnosed and managed, and how to live well with it.

Living Your Best with Early Stage Alzheimer's: An Essential Guide, Lisa Snyder, MSW, LCSW, Sunrise River Press, 2010. This book offers practical suggestions on how to talk to people about the diagnosis, daily living and for maintaining emotional and physical health.

Perspectives: A Newsletter for Individuals with Alzheimer's or a Related Disorder, Lisa Snyder, MSW, LCSW, University of California, San Diego.
This quarterly newsletter is available free of charge by email only. To subscribe: contact Lisa Snyder, at the UCSD Shiley-Marcos Alzheimer's Disease Research Center, Lsnyder@ucsd.edu.

Speaking Our Minds: What It's Like to Have Alzheimer's, Revised Edition, Lisa Snyder, MSW, Health Professions Press, 2009. The book is a collection of personal reflections from individuals with dementia and a commentary by the author.

Living Well: A Guide for Persons with Mild Cognitive Impairment (MCI) and Early Dementia, Alzheimer's Association, Minnesota and North Dakota Chapter. Information on "how life style changes can reduce and improve daily life" are presented in this workbook. Available to download: http://www.alz.org/documents/mndak/alz_living_well_workbook_web.pdf

Caregiver and Couple Memoirs

A Curious Kind of Widow: Loving a Man with Advanced Dementia, Ann Davidson, Daniel & Daniel Publishers, 2006. Personal vignettes address the difficult decisions the author had to make during the later stages of her husband's dementia.

Alzheimer's, A Love Story: One Year in My Husband's Journey, Ann Davidson, Carol Publishing, 1997. A wife's memoir describes caring for her husband with Alzheimer's disease.

An Unintended Journey: A Caregiver's Guide to Dementia, Janet Shagam, Prometheus Books, 2013. Written by a professional writer and a former caregiver for her mother, the author addresses the practical issues and challenges of being a caregiver. Frequently asked questions and worksheets are also included in each chapter.

Living with Lewy Body Dementia: One Caregiver's Personal In-depth Experience, Judy Towne Jennings, WestBow Press, 2012. The author offers an in-depth look at the cognitive, physical and emotional challenges her husband experienced throughout the stages of LBD. Many of her practical suggestions are applicable to other types of dementia.

Making an Exit: A Mother-Daughter Drama with Alzheimer's, Machine Tools, and Laughter, Elinor Fuchs, Metropolitan Books, 2005. This playwright documents her unique approach to using drama and humor to cope with her mother's dementia.

Measure of the Heart: A Father's Alzheimer's, A Daughter's Return, Mary Ellen Geist, Springboard Press, 2008. This is a beautifully written story of a daughter helping her parents in the last few years of her father's life.

Ten Thousand Joys & Ten Thousand Sorrows: A Couple's Journey Through Alzheimer's, Olivia Ames Hoblitzelle, Jeremy P. Tarcher/Penguin,Group, 2008. A wife reflects on her husband's diagnosis and 6 year journey with Alzheimer's disease, using their Buddhist teachings, poetry and philosophy to guide them. Reflection questions and comments are included with each chapter.

Through the Wilderness of Alzheimer's: A Guide in Two Voices, Robert and Anne Simpson, Augsburg Press, 1999. This book is excerpts from a couples' journal entries during the first year of his diagnosis with Alzheimer's.

Your Name Is Hughes Hannibal Shanks, Lela Knox Shanks, Penguin Books, 1999. A spouse's journey through Alzheimer's, including her valuable tips for coping and problem-solving, are included in this memoir.

Books for Families

A Caregiver's Guide to Dementia: Using Activities and Other Strategies to Prevent, Reduce and Manage Behavioral Symptoms, Laura N. Gitlin & Catherine Verrier Piersol, Camino Books, 2014. This book provides an overview of caregiving challenges, and discusses strategies to consider for various types of behavior challenges.

A Caregiver's Guide to Lewy Body Dementia, Helen Buell and Jim Whitworth, DemosHealth, 2010. This book offers a thorough overview of LBD, including chapters on diagnosis, progression, managing behaviors and health problems, and planning ahead.

A Dignified Life: The Best Friends Approach to Alzheimer's Care: A Guide for Family Caregivers, Virginia Bell and David Troxel, Health Communications, Inc., Revised edition 2012. In addition to basic information about dementia, this book describes an approach to care that focuses on being a "best friend" to the person with dementia. Helpful suggestions for communication and challenging moments are also provided.

Alzheimer's Early Stages: First Steps for Family, Friends and Caregivers, Daniel Kuhn, Hunter House, Inc., 3rd edition, 2013. The author describes early stages of Alzheimer's: issues and concerns for both the person and the family, and practical interventions for daily life.

A Pocket Guide For the Alzheimer's Caregiver, Daniel C Potts, Ellen Woodward Potts, Dementia Dynamics, LLC, 2011. Two family members who are also health care professionals address some of the common behaviors associated with Alzheimer's disease as well as self-care tips for caregivers.

An Unintended Journey: A Caregiver's Guide to Dementia, Janet Shagam, Prometheus Books, 2013. Written by a professional writer and a former caregiver for her husband, this book addresses the practical issues and challenges of being a caregiver. Frequently asked questions and worksheets are also included in each chapter.

Creating Moments of Joy for the Person With Alzheimer's or Dementia: A Journal for Caregivers, Jolene Brackey, Purdue University Press,4th edition, 2008. The author has selected "stories, quotes and dashes of humor" to encourage readers to try tools that can produce positive outcomes for care partners and for people with dementia.

Dementia with Lewy Bodies & Parkinson's Disease Dementia: Patient, Family and Clinician Working Together for Better Outcomes, J Eric Ahlskog, MD, Oxford University Press, 2014. A doctor himself, the author prepares families to talk with their relative's doctor about everyday challenges associated with Lewy Body Dementia including benefits and problems with commonly prescribed medications and dealing with cognitive and physical changes.

I'm Still Here: A New Philosophy of Alzheimer's Care, John Zeisel, Avery Press, 2010. This book focuses on the arts and dementia, creating therapeutic environments, and what it means to be a partner to someone with dementia.

Learning to Speak Alzheimer's: A Groundbreaking Approach for Anyone Dealing with the Disease, Joanne Koenig, Mariner Books, 2004. This entire book is about communication skills and learning to understand the world view of the person with dementia.

Loving Someone Who Has Dementia: How to Find Hope While Coping with Stress and Grief, Pauline Boss, Jossey-Bass, 2011. The author offers advice for care partners on dealing with the loss and grief that commonly occur while caring for someone with dementia.

Making the Connection between Brain & Behavior: Coping with Parkinson's Disease, 2nd Ed., Joseph H. Friedman, DemosHealth, 2nd edition, 2013. This handbook provides an in-depth, practical discussion of physical changes in Parkinson's Disease, changes in personality, sleep and other activities of daily life.

Navigating the Alzheimer's Journey: A Compass for Caregiving, Carol Bowlby Sifton, Health Professions Press, 2004. This comprehensive guide for caregivers includes basic information, suggestions for caregiver self care, and several chapters on creating a better quality of life for the person with dementia.

The 36 Hour Day, Nancy Mace and Peter Rabins, John Hopkins Press, 5th edition, 2011. First published in 1981, this was one of the first publications on dementia. The 5th revised edition presents up-to-date information on diagnostic evaluation, less well known types of dementia, how dementia affects the family, getting help and residential care options.

The Alzheimer's Action Plan, P. Murali Doraiswamy, M.D., Lisa Gwyther, M.S.W. and Tina Adler, St. Martin's Press, 2009. The authors answer many of the questions that they have been asked in their long and distinguished careers, starting with "What would you do if she were your mother?" Practical information on getting a diagnosis, treatment, and living with dementia are offered simply, yet thoroughly.

The Complete Guide to Alzheimer's Proofing Your Home, Mark Warner, Purdue University Press, 1999. This book discusses ways to make home caregiving safer and easier.

What if it's not Alzheimer's?: A Caregiver's Guide to Dementia with information on Frontotemporal Dementia (FTD), Lisa Radin and Gary Radin, Prometheus Books, 2007. This book provides an overview of dementia and practical strategies, but also includes several chapters specifically discussing Frontotemporal Dementia.

Where Two Worlds Touch, Jade C. Angelica, Skinner House Books, 2014. Both a personal memoir and a spiritual guide, this book discusses caring for a relative with Alzheimer's disease.

Books for Professionals

Bathing Without a Battle: Personal Care of Individuals with Dementia, Amy Louise Barrick, Springer Publishing, 2002.

Counseling People with Early Stage Alzheimer's Disease: A Powerful Process of Transformation, Robyn Yale, Health Professions Press, 2013.

Dementia and Social Work Practice: Research and Interventions, Carole B. Cox, Ed., Springer Publishing Co., 2007.

Dementia Beyond Disease: Enhancing Well-Being, G. Allen Power, Baltimore, MD: Health Professions Press. 2014.

Dementia Beyond Drugs: Changing the Culture of Care, G. Allen Power, Baltimore, MD: Health Professions Press. 2010.

Dementia Care with Black and Latino Families: A Social Work Problem-Solving Approach, Delia J Gonzalez Sanders & Richard H. Fortinsky, Springer Publishing, 2011.

Improving Hospital Care for Persons with Dementia, Nina M. Silverstein & Katie Maslow, Eds., Springer Publishing, 2005.

Practical Dementia Care, Peter Rabins and Constantine G. Lyketsos, Oxford University Press, Inc., 2nd edition, 2006.

Sexuality and Dementia: Compassionate and Practical Strategies for Dealing with Unexpected or Inappropriate Behaviors, Douglas Wornell, DemosHealth, 2013.

The Best Friend's Approach to Alzheimer's Care, Virginia Bell & David Troxel, Health Professions Press, 3rd revised printing, 2009.

The Best Friend's Staff: Building a Culture of Care in Alzheimer's Programs, Virginia Bell & David Troxel, Health Professions Press, Inc., 2001.

The End-Of Life Namaste Care Program for People with Dementia, Joyce Simard, Health Professions Press, 2nd edition, 2013.

The Enduring Self in People with Alzheimer's: Getting to the Heart of Individualized Care, Sam Fazio, Health Professions Press. 2008.

The Experience of Alzheimer's Disease: Life Through a Tangled Veil, Steven R. Sabat, Blackwell, 2001.

The Forgetting: Alzheimer's: Portrait of an Epidemic, David Shenk, Doubleday, 2001.

Whole Person Dementia Assessment, Benjamin T. Mast, Baltimore, MD: Health Professions Press, 2011.

Life Enrichment Activities

Alzheimer's Disease: Activity Focused Care, Carly Hellen, Butterworth - Heinmann, 2nd edition, 1998.

Bon Appetit: The Joy of Dining, Jitka Zgola, Health Professions Press, 2001.

Care That Works: A Relationship Approach to People with Dementia, Jitka Zgola, The Johns Hopkins University Press, 1999.

Creativity and Communication in Persons with Dementia: A Practical Guide, John Killick & Claire Craig, Jessica Kingsley Publishers, 2011.

Creative Approaches in Dementia Care, Hilary Lee & Trevor Adams, Eds., Palgrave Macmillan, 2011.

Forget Memory: Creating Better Lives for People with Dementia, Anne Basting, Johns Hopkins University Press, 2009.

Strengthen Your Mind: Activities for People Concerned About Early Memory Loss, Volume Two, Kristin Einberger & Janelle Sellick, Health Professions Press, 2008.

The Best Friends Book of Alzheimer's Activities, Volume One, Virginia Bell, David Troxel, Tonya Cox & Robin Hamon, Baltimore, MD: Health Professions Press, 2005. Second Printing.

The Best Friends Book of Alzheimer's Activities, Volume Two, Virginia Bell, David Troxel, Tonya Cox & Robin Hamon Baltimore, MD: Health Professions Press, 2007.

44192328R00080

Made in the USA
San Bernardino, CA
10 January 2017